ORIGINS OF ARCHITECTURAL PLEASURE

GRANT HILDEBRAND

ORIGINS OF ARCHITECTURAL PLEASURE

University of
California Press

Berkeley
Los Angeles
London

Credits for photographs, where other than
author, are given parenthetically in captions.

University of California Press,
Berkeley and Los Angeles, California

University of California Press, Ltd.
London, England

Library of Congress
Cataloging-in-Publication Data

Hildebrand, Grant, 1934–
Origins of architectural pleasure / Grant
Hildebrand.
p.   cm.
Includes bibliographical references and index.
ISBN 0-520-21505-2 (alk. paper)
1. Architecture—Aesthetics.
2. Architecture—Psychological aspects.
I. Title.
NA2500.H54   1999
720′.1′9—dc21   98-8213

Printed in the United States of America
9 8 7 6 5 4 3 2 1

The paper used in this publication meets the
minimum requirements of American National
Standard for Information Sciences—
Permanence of Paper for Printed Library
Materials, ANSI Z39.48-1984.

CONTENTS

The brilliance of our most recent evolutionary accretion,
the verbal abilities of the left hemisphere, obscures
our awareness of the functions of the intuitive
right hemisphere, which in our ancestors must have
been the principal means of perceiving the world.

CARL SAGAN

ACKNOWLEDGMENTS

ONE OF THE PLEASURES OF WRITING a book is that it provides the author an opportunity to thank those who have helped.

My son Matthew taught me all he could about photography. He would not be entirely happy with the work of his pupil, but it is far better than it might have been without his instruction. My son Peter read the manuscript at several stages and offered criticism and encouragement in tactful proportion.

For almost half a century Leonard Eaton has been a patient mentor, a coach, a prod, and a confidant. When I paid my meager tuition at Michigan so long ago, I had no idea that it would yield a lifelong teacher and a lifelong friend.

For several years my wife, Miriam, has stoically endured supposedly social encounters that have turned into discussions of evolution and architecture. She has endured them without protest (by and large); she has even (occasionally) encouraged them.

Gilbert Eade has repeatedly found himself drawn into those discussions. My impression is that he has not been reluctantly drawn; we share an enthusiasm for these matters. Gil's thoughts have been a continuing stimulus and sustenance to me.

Every other Monday for many years Gianna, Ginny, and Lance King, Jo Nilsson, Jack O'Connell, Arvella Wier, Miriam, and I have met for dinner. During many of those dinners we have engaged in conversations about this material that have contributed to its development. We have also shared slides of our travels, and several images in this book are from photos taken by Jo and Jack.

Marguerite Winter, a friend from college days and a recent correspondent, did all she could to remedy my ignorance about music, and offered helpful commentary on much else.

Colleagues Claus Seligmann and Jerry Finrow read the manuscript thoroughly at a key point and suggested some major reorganizations to help the sequence of the argument. Jerry arranged funding for photographic expenses. Doug Kelbaugh often stopped by to critique the work with his unique blend of wittily casual and wittily profound comments. Jeffrey Ochsner supported the work in many crucial ways at many crucial points, and secured Cory Crocker's meticulous assistance for the final preparation of the manuscript, including preparation of figures 109 and 112.

Jennifer Taylor, one of my earliest students and in recent decades Australia's foremost architectural critic, was instrumental in supporting my appointment as Chettle Fellow at the University of Sydney in 1989 to develop these ideas in an Australian classroom. She also encouraged me in the project at a subsequent time when all seemed hopeless to me.

A number of other institutions have invited me to speak on these ideas. They include the University of Winnepeg and Lawrence Technological University (1992), the University of Kobe (1993), the Walker Arts Center and the Minneapolis Chapter of the American Institute of Architects (1994), Auburn University (1994), and Pennsylvania State University (1996). The Marion Dean Ross Chapter of the Society of Architectural Historians asked me to present these ideas as Speaker of Honor for their 1996 annual meeting.

My debt to the work of other scholars is enormous. Five of them must be mentioned here. I have co-taught this material on many occasions, and have discussed it on many others, with Judi Heerwagen, psychologist, and Gordon Orians, zoologist. In the process I believe both have become friends as well as colleagues. I first heard Jay Appleton speak at the University of Washington in 1978; that talk changed the entire direction of my architectural thinking. A decade later Jay was invited as John Danz Lecturer at the university. By coincidence that was the year in which Judi, Gordon, and I first offered the course on this material; Jay assisted us in that exciting beginning. He and I have met on several occasions since, and I believe we have become warm acquaintances; my respect for his pioneering work grows with each passing year. To my regret I have never met Stephen and Rachel Kaplan, but I have profited in many and major ways from their work.

And it may well be that I have benefited most of all from the contributions of the many students, ten years of them, who have participated in the course mentioned just above.

Stephanie Fay of the University of California Press responded to my first prospectus about the manuscript with a sparkling enthusiasm, and in the same spirit has nurtured it every step of the way through editing and production processes. Nola Burger has given the book the striking and elegant look I had hoped for.

For these many supports and helps—for Miriam, and my two sons; for these remarkable friends, teachers, students, colleagues, institutions, and audiences; and for a splendid editing, design, and production staff at the Press—I am grateful beyond measure.

IN RECENT DECADES A SIZABLE LITERATURE has grown up around a study of what people like in their physical surroundings, and why. It includes such books as *The Experience of Landscape*, by Jay Appleton (1975, rev. 1996); *The Biophilia Hypothesis*, edited by Stephen R. Kellert and Edward O. Wilson (1993); *Environmental Aesthetics*, edited by Jack Nasar (1988); and *Shadows of Forgotten Ancestors*, by Carl Sagan and Ann Druyan (1992). These works are complemented by the research, observation, and speculation of other scholars, such as John Archea, Daniel Dennett, Judi Heerwagen, Nicholas Humphrey, Stephen and Rachel Kaplan, Gordon Orians, Gerd Sommerhoff, Roger Ulrich, and D. M. Woodcock. Some of them address the theoretical basis of human responses to surroundings; others have sought empirical documentation in laboratory and field; and several—this seems to be the increasing pattern—deal with both the theoretical and the empirical. All share a common ground. They are interested in the ways in which our present-day relationships to our surroundings may be influenced by those most basic and essential survival-advantageous behaviors of our early ancestors.

These scholars, by and large, examine the natural environment. The rationale for their focus is that the greater part of our species life has been spent in a natural setting. In the process of surviving and prospering we have evolved innate schemata and biologically programmed learning abilities that have supported our survival and our reproductive success in such a setting. Given the long interval between generations and our comparatively recent radical shift to an artificial environment, we might reasonably suppose that these evolved features still influence our responses. There is evidence that this is so. The psychologist Stephen Kaplan has found that when people are shown slides depicting, on the one hand, settings comprising natural materials only and, on the other, settings including humanly fabricated elements of whatever description, they uniformly prefer settings of natural materials exclusively.[1] Others corroborate Kaplan's data.[2] We can also find abundant, if more casual, evidence of our liking for natural settings in the continued popularity of such activities as camping, bicycling, hiking, skiing, fishing, and golfing, often undertaken with great effort and at considerable expense.

Yet despite such studies and recreational choices that suggest a consistent preference for natural settings, I am not entirely convinced. Comparative responses to natural settings and those including humanly constructed elements surely depend on the examples selected for comparison—we can all think of some environments, built, certainly, but natural too, to which almost any alternative would be preferable. Given some care in the selection of examples, is it possible that an artificial construct can compete with the natural in appeal? Graduate students in a class at the University of Washington, mostly from architecture but from other fields as well, in several sessions have asked test subjects to compare slides of natural settings with slides of fabricated settings selected for high visual quality. Test subjects, exclusively from fields other than design, have repeatedly found many such images equally appealing.[3] It seems reasonable to think that similar responses might be obtained outside the laboratory and classroom.[4] There is also a theoretical logic in defense of what we build, for among species that construct homes for themselves one can reasonably suppose some innate affinity for doing so; the bird must have such an affinity for its nest, the beaver for its dam. We, a species dismally equipped for self-protection, urgently require a haven against weather and predator, from which we might suspect that we are programmed to approve at least some of our building efforts to that end.

But there is no need to belabor the point, because whatever view one takes, it is obvious that purely natural settings are rare now in everyday life and are likely to remain so, while humanly constructed and composite settings are ubiquitous. Most of us, after all, are born in buildings; we live in them, go to school in them, work in them; we see plays, movies, sports events in them; we visit friends in them; we walk and drive by them every day. If we want to improve our awareness of the environment in which most of us spend most of our lives, we must in any case go beyond the natural.

Do we want to improve that awareness; is there any point in doing so? Do buildings, or the qualities of buildings, matter? Most of us hold neutral feelings about many of them, not thinking about them very much, or caring very much. Yet most of us can think too of buildings we like, or have liked; we can probably think of a few we dislike. There may even be some we hate — or love. Those for which we have the strongest feelings are often homes, our own or those of others, places in which we dwell in the usual meaning of the word. But our emotions, if not our selves, have dwelled in other types of buildings too, one way or another, at some time or other. Why do some buildings arouse in us feelings of happiness or excitement or repose? What is it in them that elicits pleasure? When we choose a new dwelling place, or build one, or make landscaping decisions for one, or for that matter occupy a workplace, select a restaurant or a table in a restaurant, plan a vacation — are there any characteristics we can identify that seem to improve our chances of contentment?

Here, paradoxically, we might draw some insights from the literature cited in the first paragraph. Although it focuses on nature, it may also help us to understand architecture. For there is reason to believe that some archetypal characteristics commonly sought in nature and essential to the lives of our remote ancestors can also find convincing architectural manifestations. We might explore this point to good purpose, asking whether those archetypal images have any creative or critical relevance to our now-ubiquitous humanly fabricated surroundings.

That is the point I want to pursue. I want to explore the literature on the survival-based appeal of certain natural characteristics to see whether it has useful architectural application. I believe the natural world that was our ancient and lengthy home may have something constructive to tell us about the architectural world that is our present and recent home.

Some caveats and conditions need to be stated.

Let me say with all possible emphasis that I do not think this approach is the only way to understand and discuss our physical surroundings, or that it is even necessarily the best way, certainly not that it should be dominant, or exclusionary, or competitive. Nor do I propose that it is universally applicable; I can think of many buildings that I and others value to which this approach can contribute little. I do think, however, that in a number of cases it can offer useful insights, that there is an abundance of recent work in many cognate fields that might inform it, and that for these reasons it merits attention. It is an attempt to introduce a new point of view toward some aspects of architectural experience. I hope it will be seen as a complementary way of understanding.

The core of the argument I explore here derives from the relationships that some characteristics of our surroundings, natural and artificial, may bear to some of our innate survival-supportive behaviors. A respectable defense can be made for this approach. It can claim a degree of external support from an abundance of investigation and observation by the scholars mentioned in the first paragraph of this introduction and by many others. It is the approach scientists use in studying habitat selection by other animals; there is some prima facie reason to ask whether it says anything about Homo sapiens's choices in that matter. It is also supported by the principle of reasonable probability, for while no one would suggest that all or even a majority of our responses to our surroundings are necessarily innate, the probability that some are influenced by our genetic constitution is overwhelming. This approach also has the merit of simplicity: it aids an understanding of some characteristics of architectural settings with a relative economy and clarity of argument.

This approach is intentionally founded on our current understanding of various issues of evolution. Although some of the experiential principles I suggest here might be argued from observation and empirical data alone, an evolutionary basis can provide a usefully higher level of abstraction for exploring them; it can help to shape questions for further examination; it can provide a theoretical road map for further development. Hence its value. And if we set aside the controversy in some quarters about the very concept of evolution, there is fairly widespread agreement about many of its larger constituent issues; the early thorny question of a mechanism through which evolution could work, for example, was answered in the mid twentieth century by the discovery of DNA and genetic transmittal. Nevertheless, many smaller matters of interpretation, and a few large ones as well, are seriously disputed and probably will be for a long time to come.

I write, however, as an architect, with no credentials in archaeology, psychology, biology, or zoology, and certainly none in music or poetry. Each of those fields comprises a body of knowledge with which I can hope for only a superficial familiarity. But if I am to tackle the relationship of architecture to the various issues and interpretations of evolution, I must try to follow controversies centered in those fields and must choose among competing positions. Sometimes this is not difficult. Sometimes positions that purport to differ widely do not. Where real differences exist, however, no position can claim an absolute proof; if it could, there would be no alternative positions to evaluate. So judgments must be made. Fortunately there are criteria a lay observer can ponder. Advocates of various positions will argue, typically, an internal consistency and logic, especially in the face of challenge, and will claim support from physical observation, psychological insight regarding ourselves and other animals, and physiological facts. Advocates of some positions increasingly claim support from empirical data, game theory, and computer simulation. In deciding between positions, one can evaluate the solidity of each of these arguments and claims. I have done so by the obvious means: I have read all I can about the positions themselves, along with rebuttals, commentaries, and critiques, with an emphasis on more recent publications. After doing this, in all cases I have consulted a colleague or friend who is closer to the material professionally. Having done these things, sometimes repeatedly, I have accepted what seems the more convincing position on any given issue — which has not always turned out to be the most popularly conspicuous position. I have especially benefited from extended co-teaching and discussion with my colleagues Judi Heerwagen, a psychologist, and Gordon Orians, a zoologist. Among many writers and speakers whose works have been particularly helpful I would cite Jay Appleton, Daniel Dennett, Stephen and Rachel Kaplan, Carl Sagan, Roger Ulrich, and Robert Wright. Of these I have talked personally only with Jay Appleton (extensively) and Roger Ulrich (very briefly). Inevitably there are instances in which I have poorly understood, or misunderstood, or misapplied the work of these and other scholars. In all such instances the fault is likely to be mine much more than theirs.

Inevitably too, readers who already hold a position on one issue or another are likely to find that their choice is not in every case the one endorsed. But in the absence of consensus on these matters, if the subject is to be approached at all, it is hard to see how else to begin; if I enumerated most of the arguments pro and con regarding each point, the resultant book would be unreadable; it would probably be unwritable. I try throughout to state each issue straightforwardly, to draw architectural inferences from it in the same spirit, and to point to the germane features of illustrative examples. I try to summarize straightforwardly the pertinent background of theoretical and empirical support as I understand it. Those who find this approach inadequate, and those who believe that a position is unconvincingly or erroneously presented, can often find an expanded discussion in the notes, along with the sources on which my comments in the text are founded. Those sources and the bibliography, with the bibliographies of the works in it, represent a further wealth of additional research, observation, and explication, much of it recent, for those who choose to pursue it.

This approach, though it has been associated with environmental determinism and quantifiable objectivity, is neither. It seeks to explore material that with further attention might make a useful contribution to architectural judgment. It does not supply proofs, nor does it supply quantifiable absolute norms. It cannot. As my discussion of archetypes in the next chapter should make plain, any exact specification for the characteristics explored here would be evolutionarily unworkable, for at least two fundamental reasons. Individuals differ, and quite widely too; but even were this not so, environments themselves always differ from one another in space and time, and choices among them are inevitably based on the best options immediately available. Yet although this approach thus does not seek and cannot provide quantifiable objectivity, its observations can inform architectural judgment. There is a recognizable and significant difference between a horizontal plane a handspan above one's head and one at two or three times human height; likewise a dark space contiguous to a brightly lit one is recognizably different from two contiguous spaces of equal brightness; and there is reason to offer some meaningful observations about general preferences in such matters. But it is not pragmatically or theoretically possible — nor do I think it desirable — to talk in either case of feet and inches, centimeters, or foot-candles. This inquiry seeks, not quantifiable specifications, but an increased qualitative understanding of the underlying predilections we all share, on which individual and cultural experiences are densely overlaid to introduce infinite nuances and variations.

How do we choose examples for discussion? If we are to look at buildings and settings we like to examine why we like them, how do we derive a useful list of examples that are liked? One method, widely used, is to examine the responses of representative subject groups to slides of various settings. From time to time I draw on this method, both as I have used it occasionally in my own classes and, much more important, as it has been used in the work of other, far more skilled, researchers. Another method samples paintings and literature that record settings appealing to the painter or writer. This method too I intend to use occasionally in minor and supportive instances, drawing from my own observations and those of colleagues. Yet another method examines buildings or settings that can be shown to have been remarkably satisfying — or, as negative evidence, unsatisfying — to past or present-day occupants. I intend to use this approach too on occasion.

Yet another way of going about the task is to identify an array of buildings and settings that people spend considerable time and money to experience. They spend time and money to place themselves in natural settings, as I have already noted, but they just as certainly spend it to place themselves in settings that include buildings or are buildings — clearly this expenditure is one pragmatic criterion of a building's attractiveness value. It is also a criterion that raises real questions of validity and requires some fine-tuning. For people spend time and money to visit buildings for reasons other than architectural appeal. Touring coaches crowd around Notre-Dame de Paris, for example, not just because of its architectural delights but also because of its celebration in literature and movies and its centrality to a city in which one can dine and shop remarkably well. Lincoln's birthplace is visited for none of these reasons, but because it is Lincoln's birthplace. To avoid the objections such examples suggest, I have tried to pick examples that are independent of other attractions, that are visited just for their architectural selves. If one could also object that some buildings that meet these criteria are visited primarily because they are starred in the guidebooks, I would answer that there may be considered and long-term reasons, however various, for the guidebook stars. It seems constructive to ask whether these reasons involve some characteristics, shared among examples, that might in part explain the guidebook stars.

If all these considerations are addressed in the selection of examples, the results have some describable advantages. As many researchers have shown, design professionals differ from lay observers in their reactions to architectural examples, or to landscape examples for that matter. The proposed criterion, however, sidesteps the point by selecting examples with a record of appeal to both groups. As such it tells us less about differences between lay and professional, but it may tell us more about characteristics valued by both. If in addition we use as test examples buildings people have long spent time and money to visit, we ought to transcend the effects of transitory taste inherent in the responses of present-day audiences or, for that matter, the momentary enthusiasms of some earlier painter or poet. If we give special attention to buildings and settings valued by many people who are not of the cultures that created those buildings and settings, moreover, we may transcend cultural distinctions as well.[5] If, then, as this book proposes, we wish to discover some deep-running, perhaps quasi-universal likes and dislikes in our architectural surroundings, this way of choosing test cases may be a relatively good one. I intend to use it widely here: most buildings and settings used as examples in this book are ones that many people, lay and professional, of many cultures and many times, have made a considerable effort to see.

That methodology, however, suggests that examples are going to be drawn from a fairly distant past. Few would dispute that the inclusion of recent buildings and settings would make the discussion more interesting, and probably more useful. But the criteria I have described work less well for recent examples: the poets and painters have not had their chance; occupants have not yet recorded likes and dislikes; and although some recent examples may have generated a reputation as rewarding destinations in themselves, the "test of time" has just begun. For recent work I have generally picked examples endorsed in serious critical journalism and, for very recent work, those structures given significant professional recognition. I realize these criteria open other objections, but so do any alternatives.

Examples represent five continents and five—almost six—millennia. They are organized without regard to chronological or geographic order, according to the role they play in the narrative, to explore more freely the extent to which the characteristics and principles these examples illustrate span cultures and centuries. Some readers will be quick to notice that there are few vernacular examples and few from eras of technological infancy. Given the theme of this book, that may seem odd. I discuss the reasons for these omissions at the end of the book, where they make the most sense; those who need an earlier explanation can turn to those concluding remarks at any time.

Most pictorial representations in this book are photographs of groups of buildings, building exteriors, and building interiors. As books on architecture go, there are few plans and sections. I generally omit them because I am attempting to deal with what happens to us, what our responses are, as we experience buildings, and at such times we see the buildings themselves and not diagrams. Even so, when discussions depend on information that only a plan or section can provide, I include one or both.

Of course reliance on pictorial representation itself raises a problem. In a book such as this we attempt to understand three-dimensional spaces by looking at two-dimensional images. Yet a two-dimensional image is not the same as three-dimensional immersion. This distinction will trouble some readers, and with some reason. I admit that when actually visiting a place for the first time I find surprises, no matter how much I might have studied two-dimensional material beforehand. But I would add that where such study has been serious and detailed, the surprises have been few, and there is evidence that this is generally the case: "Studies which have compared photos versus actual trips to a site show that responses do not vary significantly as a function of presentation format."[6] Nevertheless, many observations put forward here no doubt do depend on camera location, light quantity and direction, perhaps even photographic film and developing. What to do? Even if I were to include a videotape of examples recorded through movement in space, the retina—yours and mine—would still be looking at two-dimensional images, though admittedly we would be looking at quite a lot of them. The argument is muddied still more by the often useful realizations we can draw from an image regardless of its authenticity of representation. A photo or drawing that represents actuality quite inaccurately, or is even a contrivance never to be experienced in real life, may still have a good bit to tell us through our reactions to it. Eugene Smith's famous photograph *The Walk to Paradise Garden* (see figure 12) is an example: we can discuss its appeal as an image on the retina per se without regard to its accurate representation of any actuality we encounter in real life. Still, for architectural illustrations I have tried to choose reasonably representative views; most photos are my own, taken with ordinary cameras, normal lenses, and natural lighting. I have walked most of these places; the impressions I describe seem to me to come from the settings themselves. I hope both that readers will augment these impressions with their own, and that those impressions will bear a reasonable kinship to the ones offered here.

I illustrate each principle I discuss in a deliberately concise selection of architectural examples, enough, I hope, to make my point while avoiding tedium. I do not mean, however, to invite the conclusion that each principle applies to only a few examples. To discourage that conclusion, I often mention a number of other buildings or families of buildings in which the principle under discussion can be seen. I hope each reader will extend the list, adding personal instances based on individual experience. But I do not intend to encourage the opposite view, that examples like those discussed are necessarily commonplace. They are not. In one way and another we have conferred a specialness on these settings. In asking why this has happened, we may find that they have something to tell us about the constitution of specialness.

1
A meadow, woods, a stream, and cows, somewhere in England.

THIS SCENE PRESENTS TO OUR EYE an array of natural material: we seem to be standing at the edge of a wooded embankment; below lies a sunlit meadow, bounded by distant edges of the wood; a few examples of domesticated animal life are strewn around the meadow; diagonally at right is what looks to be a quiet stream.

Most of us are likely to have encountered something similar at one time or another, and most of us will have found the experience pleasant, so much so that we may have felt an urge to linger at such a place, without thought of time, indeed without wishing to think of anything other than the beauty of the moment. If we seek a mood at all in such a setting, it is likely to be that of Melville's mastheader, whose "spirit ebbs away to whence it came; becomes diffused through time and space," or that "serene and blessed mood" recalled by Wordsworth in which

2
The Onrin-do,
Katsura, Kyoto,
1620 – 45.

> with an eye made quiet by the power
> Of harmony, and the deep power of joy,
> We see into the life of things.

Another scene, this one with an architectural component: the Onrin-do in the gardens of the Katsura Villa at Kyoto. The small temple presents to us a generous shadowed opening; above is the palpable shelter of the heavy tiled roof. The temple is sited so that its more distant parts are withdrawn into a dense wood embracing the temple on either side; it faces a small clearing that falls away to the water's edge. Ahead is the extensive sunlit expanse of the water's surface, a narrow inlet of which is crossed by the bridge. This scene too is strangely appealing, and is so in, again, a particularly innate and languorous way.

A third example, purely architectural: the vista toward the nave from the side aisle of Orvieto cathedral. The aisle is relatively dark; the nave beyond, seen through the screen of columns, is brightened by the sunlight streaming through the unseen window. The image is

3
Orvieto cathedral,
1290–1420. A view
from the side aisle
toward the nave.

imbued with repetitive patterns: the striped masonry of the piers, repeated in the wall in the distance, the details of the stringcourse under the windows, the rhythm of the roof trusses, themselves elaborately configured. This building is of sufficient appeal that it has been a pilgrimage destination for many over a long period of time, and most would probably consider this representation of it an attractive one.

Each of these scenes—nature, nature and architecture, architecture—also presents a number of characteristics important to the survival of early members of our species. It is possible to suggest a relationship between the appeal these scenes hold for us and the survival-advantage characteristics they embody; each may usefully contribute to our understanding of the other. This book explores that possibility.

THE AESTHETICS
OF SURVIVAL

CREATURES WHOSE BEHAVIORS HELP THEM to live long enough to procreate, who also reproduce most effectively and most effectively care for their offspring, on average will get more offspring into the next generation than those whose behaviors are less supportive. Their offspring, in turn, equipped with the same instincts, are likely to behave similarly, and so will beget and raise yet another especially abundant contribution to the ensuing generation. The biologist's term for this process is "natural selection"; the characteristics of those individuals who exhibit such advantageous behaviors in the greatest degree are "selected for." Conversely, those characteristics of individuals that contribute less to survival and reproductive success tend to vanish over time; they are "selected against." Thus natural selection supports and enhances traits that confer advantages for survival and reproduction. This point is central to Darwin's mid-nineteenth-century thesis, which, challenged and modified over many decades, has been confirmed in its general stance and broad outlines and continues to be confirmed by a multitude of experiments and observations.[1]

There is now general agreement, however, that for most creatures evolution is not a smoothly continuous process but involves occasional episodes of "rapid" change interspersed with far longer periods of stasis.[2] But there is a good bit of contention about how we should interpret the terms "rapid" and "longer." This contention seems to me to be largely a matter of emphasis. Those who stress the rapidity of evolutionary change emphasize that in geologic time, change may be "instantaneous," by which is meant perhaps one hundred thousand years, perhaps no more than the thickness of an onion skin in fossil strata. Those who emphasize a gradual interpretation point out that such a rate of change presents no noticeable differences in the species at issue measured against all of recorded human history.[3] Whatever the temporal emphasis, in everyday terms most creatures, including ourselves, have experienced enormously lengthy periods in which their genetic future is served by inherent characteristics, little changed from generation to generation, that have been whetted toward survival advantages over millennia, even aeons.[4] By such measures the period in which we have been elsewhere than Africa is brief; the period in which most of us have been other than hunters and gatherers is briefer still; the period in which we have been primarily urban dwellers is the blink of an eye.

But what initiates survival-advantageous behavior in the individual creature? In particular—since our interest here is the relationship of creatures, and especially ourselves, to the immediate physical environment—from whence arise the complex survival-advantageous responses of creatures to their surroundings?

Some responses result from individual cognitive processes: the creature acquires ideas about the environment from parents or other adults of the species, from peers, or from individual experience. In the animal world Konrad Lorenz has studied early experiences that instill predilections retained throughout the creature's life; he has called this process imprinting. In Homo sapiens predilections resulting from early experience or instruction may drive elements of our behavior throughout our lives. "There is always one moment in childhood when the door opens and lets the future in,"[5] says Graham Greene, which we might amend to include many moments, many doors, and many versions of a future. Because of the context in which it was first or repeatedly experienced, a particular natural setting, a room, a sound, a smell, even certain architectural characteristics, may retain associations, may shape choices, throughout the life of an individual. Such associations, retained, examined, modified in greater or lesser degree, affect our most personal likes and dislikes; they are primary causes of individual taste.[6] When we say tastes differ, or there is no accounting for taste, we are probably referring to responses in this realm, responses that come from individual experience or instruction.

Other responses are common among compatriots in place and time: shared customs, forms, beliefs, associations and values, ways of reasoning, ways of prioritizing, and ways of building constitute the material that makes a culture cohere.[7] These characteristics too evolve through time, distinguishing a culture at one time from the "same" culture at another time.

These two realms of response—the individual and the culturally influenced—are important forces informing the behavior of our own species in present-day life; certainly the two realms together account for an enormous array of behaviors and thoughts we now manifest and ideas we utilize.

Some behaviors of all creatures, however, come neither from imparted knowledge, personal experience, nor enculturation. Some are in place at the moment the creature becomes an active individual being. The female of several varieties of wasp lays the fertilized egg in an underground nest and never returns. The young wasp, emerging at the proper time, lives a life identical to that of the parent, obviously without postpartum instruction. The cuckoo leaves its egg in the nest of another species; the chick, after hatching, immediately pushes the host's eggs from the nest, thereby securing all the nurturing attention of the host. This behavior is enacted at the beginning of life, generation after generation, with no postpartum instruction whatever — quite the opposite, in fact, since the surrogate parent is always of another species, whose behavior is not at all that of the cuckoo. Another type of genetically carried behavior appears later in the creature's life, and here again we can turn to the cuckoo for an example common to many higher animals: the cuckoo "knows" it is a cuckoo; when it becomes an adult, it mates only with other cuckoos. If this were not the case, there would be no new cuckoos to continue the story.

> The honeybee scout returns to the hive from a foraging expedition and "dances," rapidly crawling in a particular, fairly complex pattern over the honeycomb . . . , her motions monitored by the spectators through their sense of touch. Given only this information, a swarm of bees then flies out of the hive in the proper direction to the proper distance to a food supply they've never visited as effortlessly as if this was their daily, familiar commute from home to work.[8]

Such innate behaviors occasionally extend even into the realm of aesthetics:

> Given pencils and paints, chimps with considerable drive and deliberation make art that, though exclusively nonrepresentational as far as we can see, is thought presentable in some circles. Male bower birds decorate their nests guided by an aesthetic that resonates with ours; they regularly replace picked flowers, feathers, and fruit that are no longer fresh; their art evolves through the summer. Gibbons fling themselves balletically through the high forests, and chimps can be counted on to rock and roll at waterfalls and rainstorms. Chimps delight in resonant drumming, and gibbons in song.[9]

But are these decoratings and flingings and drummings really enacted automatically, or does the creature learn these behaviors from others of the species? It is hard to say in the specific behaviors described in the quotation. But even if experiments offered an answer, the question itself opens another issue. We have known for some time that in many creatures certain characteristics arise from a combination of sources: there is a genetic program for learning built into the creature, and there is also some postpartum teaching-and-learning event that enacts the program. Lorenz's experiments document such teaching and learning as it is programmed to occur at certain times for certain creatures without, apparently, other restrictions; whatever happened to his creatures in the crucial time period was imprinted as a behavior. Programmed options available in other instances and for other creatures, however, may be much more closely controlled. The chaffinch, for example, does not automatically sing a finch's song when it becomes an adult—but it is programmed to learn that song and readily responds to singing lessons offered, also innately, by other chaffinches. But it responds only to a finch-song curriculum; no matter how extensively "taught," it will not learn the nightingale's tune.[10] This phenomenon—a behavior that must be taught and learned but for which a learning structure is lodged in the genetic material—is now termed biologically prepared learning.

What of Homo sapiens? Certain obviously innate behaviors are evident at the earliest stages of individual human life: "One does not learn to feel afraid or to cry any more than one learns to feel pain or to gasp for air. . . . Five emotions can be elicited at birth. . . . There is no evidence to suggest that feelings are necessarily preceded by a cognitive process."[11] Fear of falling, for example, does not appear to result from early imprinting, cognitive learning, or parent-imparted information, nor is it enculturated; it is found in earliest infant life and in all cultures.[12] It can be overcome by mental processes—the paratrooper or skydiver can override it in this way—but it does not just go away; it remains part of our being to such an extent that the term "ineradicable" is fully justified. There is good reason for its presence and persistence. Among creatures vulnerable to injury or death by falling, those who are innately careful where falls are likely improve their chances of reaching reproductive age. Their genetic line will, in that respect, be selected for. A fear-of-falling response perpetuates itself, as do all such useful innate predilections. Among characteristics that appear in us at a later stage in life the most obvious are copulative desire and ability. They appear in us as in other species at a predictable time and with an elaborate accompaniment of related behaviors; they appear without conscious formal adult or peer instruction and without cognitive reflection and are neither easily repressed nor easily modified by such means, as we now know too well. Of the third family of genetically dependent behaviors it now seems that we have a truly astonishing example: there is now some evidence that our urge to invent, learn, and develop language, and our ability to do so, may be determined and enabled by an extraordinarily extensive genetically carried program for the acquisition of linguistic ability.

We can thus identify three families of responses and behaviors built into the genetic material of many creatures, including ourselves: those immediately operative from the moment of the creature's appearance as an active individual being, those that occur spontaneously at a later time in life, and those that drive and shape biologically prepared learning.

In our species the range of such innate responses must be unusually extensive. This is not just a cavalier or anthropocentric view. Genetically programmed responses are largely determined by the limbic brain, whose evolution to unusual size in our species is now thought to predate the later enlargement of the cortex.[13] The responses shaped by Homo sapiens's limbic brain had to be extensive through harsh necessity, because they had to see us through aeons of early species life without the aid of much of the built-in defensive and offensive equipment that has helped other species. We have neither horns nor good claws, nor shell, nor effective fighting teeth, nor venom; we have no fur to protect us from the cold; we cannot move very far, or very fast; we are poor swimmers and we cannot fly at all. We are of modest size; we are poorly camouflaged. Our smell and hearing are marginal compared to those of many species; our sight is less acute than that of many birds of prey, and we lack some mechanisms of visual perception found in birds, insects, and fish. "Feeble and almost defenseless primates," Carl Sagan calls us.[14] The limbic brain has governed behaviors that have enabled us to cope despite this multitude of deficiencies. When we include all such immediately necessary behaviors, we have for our species an impressively large body of innate material. When we add to it an unknown number of innate predilections for genetically prepared learning, including those that lead us to invent and develop and utilize language, we have a massive body of innate material indeed.

But "innate predilections" is a cold and clumsy term for the complex activating mechanisms behind human intuitive behaviors. We can more simply say that the real motivators are pleasure and relief from discomfort. There is no reason to think that early Homo sapiens engaged in sexual activity knowing offspring would result; the behavior was undertaken for pleasure, as it still is. "Lust and other such feelings are natural selection's way of getting us to act as if we wanted lots of offspring and knew how to get them, whether or not we actually do."[15] But what of our behavior when confronted with conditions, suggested earlier, in which a fatal fall is a real possibility? There the issue is not exactly pleasure; it is more a matter of relief of discomfort. We are uncomfortable near such conditions; we step back from the cliff's edge because we feel a lot better away from that potentially fatal zone. Even when we test such fear, it remains as a protecting element. Ingestion combines the motivations: we eat and drink both to relieve discomfort and to obtain pleasure. We enact these and innumerable other helpful behaviors without analytical examination; we behave in these ways because we want to. We have an inarticulate but insistent urge. We feel better when we obey it.

In a quite real sense, natural selection "designs" creatures over time by the harsh culling processes of evolution, favoring those whose innate preferences—whose "likes"—better the chances of a genetic future. It has "designed" us, in that same sense, to like certain conditions and experiences in preference to others.[16]

So the premise: in reflecting on the various settings and experiences of our lives, we should be able to find some fairly close matches between characteristics we like and characteristics that would have improved our chances of survival.

As recently as ten thousand years ago worldwide, and much more recently in most geographic regions, we depended on responses to the features of an environment made up of almost entirely natural material. It is not surprising that natural material can still stimulate similar responses in us; given our long generational cycle, it would be more surprising to find that we embody significantly different preferences over what is, evolutionarily, a brief span of time. But we are justified in thinking that similar responses may be stimulated by phenomena and artifacts fabricated by ourselves? Is it valid to speak of these as analogous to natural conditions?

Individual natural settings always differ from one another in some degree. No two groves, caves, meadows, or streams are exactly alike. Furthermore, Heraclitus long ago pointed out the inevitable change over time in any grove, cave, meadow, or stream. So the response-generating characteristics of any particular setting cannot be so specific as to be unique to that example at that moment—if they were, we would respond only to that specific place and time and would be unresponsive to the advantages or dangers of similar settings or even, for that matter, the same setting at a different moment or from a different viewpoint. Such a basis for intuitive survival response would be evolutionarily unworkable. The characteristics that drive our responses, then, must exist as images within us in some degree of abstraction.[17] We do not seek only a particular bend in a particular river at a particular never-to-be-repeated moment, as seen from an exact vantage point, and ignore all similar manifestations. Rather we must be attuned to the sound of rivers generally, the glistening character of light reflecting from them, the presence or absence of prey or predator in them or along their banks, the vegetation that edges them. We respond appropriately—with delight, interest, boredom, revulsion, or fear—to infinite permutations of such conditions. The image in us that stimulates our approach to any particular river, our sense that we like or dislike this place, that we find it beautiful or repulsive—such an image must be in the nature of an archetypal abstraction. Any particular place at any moment will be a greater or lesser manifestation of this archetypal image; no particular place will uniquely manifest it. If this is the case, and it is hard to see how it can be otherwise, it must follow that the characteristics of the archetype may not be exclusive to nature. We are entitled to ask whether they may be found in artificial phenomena and artifacts as well. What would seem to count is not whether the image that presents itself to the senses is natural or artificial, but whether it adequately presents to those senses the characteristics of the archetypal image.[18]

I seek such archetypal characteristics in what I have called and will call settings, particular identifiable places of describable and limited extent, consisting of natural and artificial materials in any configuration or combination, but with emphasis on the fabricated component, the architectural component. I ask whether and to what degree archetypal characteristics with survival value can be discerned in settings, and especially architectural settings, of unusual appeal.

What is the point of doing so? Why should this be of any interest?

Over the years many theories have been put forward to promote or defend or explain particular characteristics of the settings in which we live. Those theories have never been accompanied by a clear chain of reasoning to support the claims of value made or implied for them. As an example, Leon Battista Alberti in the fifteenth century argued that architecture, and by implication town form, should build on principles of the ancient Greco-Roman architectural tradition; a century later Palladio argued much the same point. Both believed that adhering to such principles would have some positive value for the observer; neither showed how or why others should believe this. To take a completely different example, Frank Lloyd Wright in the twentieth century claimed that in his residential designs he had "destroyed the box," without saying why the world should value that achievement. It may well be that these or any of a hundred other such architectural characteristics are in some way meaningful to us; but if so, how and why? A survival-advantage approach in some cases may suggest answers to such questions. It may suggest ways to reframe some of the questions; it may suggest the value of linking discussions of some such architectural issues to the considerable body of theory and empirical investigation centered on human nature and human behavior. By such means it can, in fact, lead to observations about, among other things, both the Greco-Roman vocabulary and Wright's destruction of the box. But it can also move the discussion from the particular examples to general principles embodied in each, thereby pointing to creative new interpretations of those principles, interpretations quite independent of the examples used to illustrate them.

This approach holds another promise: by its nature it should pertain to all members of our species. From a historical point of view we should be able to illustrate its principles in settings from vastly different times, geographies, and cultures, each with its own language and level of technical sophistication; we should find, in turn, that existing examples appeal to people from equally differing times, geographic origins, and cultures with different languages and levels of technical sophistications.[19] We might hope too that we could go beyond the extant, that applying this approach in new work might yield an equal catholicity of appeal.[20]

Others have suggested such a survival-advantage approach to the general question of sensory appeal. Nicholas Humphrey quotes from the Scottish philosopher Thomas Reid, who, in 1785 — in a statement preceding Darwin's *Origin of Species* by more than seventy years — suggested that modern biologists,

> by a careful examination of the objects which Nature hath given this amiable quality [of beauty], . . . may perhaps discover some real excellence in the object, or at least some valuable purpose that is served by the effect it produces upon us. This instinctive sense of beauty, in different species of animals, may differ as much as the external sense of taste, and in each species be adapted to its manner of life.[21]

So too John Dewey in 1934, in *Art as Experience*, pursued the idea of primordial purpose behind the aesthetic experience:

> The nature of experience is determined by the essential conditions of life. While man is other than bird and beast, he shares basic vital functions with them and has to make the same basal adjustments if he is to continue the process of living. Having the same vital needs, man derives the means by which he breathes, moves, looks and listens, the very brain with which he coordinates his senses and his movements, from his animal forebears. . . .
> . . . the one who sets out to theorize about the esthetic experience embodied . . . must begin with it in the raw.[22]

Marc-Antoine Laugier in the mid eighteenth century and Gottfried Semper in the mid nineteenth suggested that such an approach might be pertinent to architecture: Semper wrote, "I see myself forced to go back to the primitive conditions (*Urzustände*) of human society."[23] Most recently Michael Benedikt, addressing a somewhat different purpose, has considered architecture as "re-creating, re-collecting, re-constructing and re-producing the structures of the vital settings and situations of our primeval past." He continues in words that deserve quoting:

> It is instructive to recall that all of Architecture, which we usually take to begin in earnest some nine thousand years B.C., represents no more than one five-hundredth of the time mammals have been extant. During this seminal period, the essential elements of advantage accorded by certain patterns — figures — of shelter construction and site selection were becoming a part of *all* living and surviving. . . . how many of what we take to be specifically modern problems emerge with general form intact from this unimaginably long terrestrial history. . . . Paths of pursuit, places of surveillance, concavities for shelter, locations of food; traps, strongholds, graves . . . these, like drought and flood, are ecological givens common to all living things. Given too, and simultaneously, are the significance of high places and low places, light places and dark places, near places and distant ones, of inside and outside, cold and warm. . . . The meanings of these places, far from "culturally assigned" or free for the invention, are givens for animals no less than people; givens, for all intents and purposes, no less reliable than any natural physical law.[24]

How do we explore further the given meanings of our surroundings?

If we are to have a good chance of survival success, we must be highly competent at four basic activities: ingestion, procreation, the securing of appropriate habitation, and exploration. The first two have a few architectural implications, but those of greatest interest to this book are really subsumed in the characteristics of the habitat. We come then, rather quickly, to the matter of securing appropriate habitation. That activity is architectural in its essence; appropriate habitation in its broadest interpretation is what architecture has always been entirely about. I am going to begin, then, by considering the key issue first: what must appropriate habitation for Homo sapiens provide? I will then turn to the less obvious but equally interesting question of the exploration of our environment, to see whether there are any architectural characteristics that may be germane to that behavior. Having got that far, I am going to change course a bit to reflect on some architectural manifestations of two conjoined characteristics that are fundamental to all four of our survival activities.

FINDING A
GOOD HOME

AMONG CREATURES WHO HAVE TO FIND OR MAKE HOMES, natural selection rewards those who do it well. We, Homo sapiens, have chosen by intuition among habitats offered by nature, and by intuition we have built. We were selected—rather strongly, apparently—for an innate ability to choose good habitats over bad, and an innate predilection to build in some ways rather than others.

A Home in Nature

There are different views about the larger geographic locale in which earliest Homo sapiens lived, but in any case the immediate small-scale setting would have ranged from dense wood to savanna. Such settings allowed us to thrive; we must have been attuned to them. Without yet asking in detail what specific things were particularly supportive, we note the obvious: those early homes—like all our surroundings until the last few millennia—comprised entirely natural material; they were places of sheltering and edible green and growing things, of water, of prey and predator, the seasons, sun and storm. It is thus easy to see a basis for the findings of Stephen Kaplan and others that we prefer natural scenes.[1] As the psychologist Roger Ulrich has said, "We are biologically predisposed to liking scenes with prominent natural elements."[2] It is thus also easy to explain the ubiquitous choice, among those who could choose, of a dwelling in an extensive natural surrounding as the ideal setting for a satisfying life. One could cite the patrician villas of republican and imperial Rome, Roman and post-Roman Britain, and Japan; the baroque retreats of the French aristocracy; the palaces and gardens of Islam's Umayyad and Abassid princes. Still today "the wealthy will continue to seek dwellings on prominences above water amidst parkland,"[3] while a country vacation—a trip to the mountains or the beach, to a trout stream or an island—is universally considered a valued adjunct to everyday life.

> The gardens of merchants in medieval Chinese cities indicate that early urban peoples went to considerable lengths to maintain contact with nature. During the last two centuries, in several countries, the idea that exposure to nature fosters psychological well-being, reduces the stresses of urban living, and promotes physical health has formed part of the justification for providing parks and other nature in cities and preserving wilderness for public use.[4]

So too we often idealize the natural. The painters of the Hudson River school and of the American West, Gauguin on Tahiti, even to some extent books such as *All Creatures Great and Small*, magazines such as *National Geographic*, movies such as *Greystoke*, in varying degrees celebrate and romanticize our affinity with nature.

When we cannot actually place ourselves in a natural setting, we are willing to make some effort to provide ourselves with substitutes. Studies by the psychologist Judi Heerwagen find that while people generally put striking natural scenes on their walls, those who work in windowless spaces do so much more consistently and predictably (figure 4).

Satisfying this affinity can have a measurable effect on mental and physical well-being. Roger Ulrich has shown that views of natural scenes bring about a reduction in stress among university students facing a challenging exam and that a view to a natural setting, or even a picture representing a natural setting, significantly shortens recovery time for surgical pa-

4
The surrogate
natural setting
(© Judith Heerwagen).

tients in hospital recovery rooms. He cites studies by colleagues showing that prison inmates with views to nature report for sick call less frequently than those without such views.[5] Other research shows that the intuitive custom of bringing flowers to hospital patients improves their rate of recovery. Flowers are widely understood to offer pleasure—there can be no real doubt that they contribute to the appeal of figure 5—and they have been themes of architectural ornamentation around the globe and across time (figure 6).

> For an organism that rarely eats flowers, it is perhaps surprising that we place such a high value on them and spend so much effort and money to have flowers in and around our dwellings and in city parks. The evolutionary biologist, however, sees flowers as signals of improving resources and as providing cues about good foraging sites some time in the future. In species-rich plant communities, flowers also provide the best way to determine the locations of plants that offer different resources. . . . Thus, paying attention to flowers should result in improved functioning in natural environments.[6]

Similarly, architectures in obvious close rapport with living nature may appeal for that reason. The shrine buildings of Ise (figure 7), made of natural materials and folded into the

5
Wells cathedral,
Somerset, 1174–1460.
A nave pier.

6
Exeter cathedral,
Devon, 1270–1470.
Flowers in the
vaulting.

glades of the cryptomeria forest, are immediately and intuitively understood as reiterations of the elemental dwelling, and as such they are appropriate to the Shinto philosophy of which they are an expression. But such an understanding is not restricted to those familiar with Shinto; the buildings declare their references to any observer. The materials are meticulously worked and finished with unequaled refinement, yet at completion they retain many characterists of their natural state: dominant wood members, like the trees from which they came, are cylinders, vertically disposed; their length is many times a multiple of their diameter; like all the wood of the shrines, they retain the coloration of untreated wood. In color and pattern, the thatch, especially in the weathered state it reaches a few years after each re-building, resembles the reeds and grasses from which it came. Similar associations suggest themselves in the early-twentieth-century wooden buildings done by Greene and Greene, Bernard Maybeck, and Ernest Coxhead in the San Francisco Bay Area: the slopes of soft-edged rafters suggest arboreal branchings; ubiquitous shingles abstract the texture and color of tree bark. A similar rapport—perhaps a similar archetypal evocation would be the better phrase—characterizes some much more recent work in the American Pacific Northwest (figure 8).

Changing the material does not necessarily change the message. Some nineteenth-century authors proposed that the Gothic was a conscious emulation of the forest grove; we now think such explanations naive, but there may be an analogous effect on the viewer. The chapter house of Wells, for example (figure 9), or the palm-vaulted nave of Exeter (see figure 6) so strongly evoke a woodland glade that it is easy to believe the pleasure we find in either structure arises from a correspondence to an archetypal image. To change the material once again, the Tokyo architect Kazunari Sakamoto has recently done a series of buildings with undulating steel roofs on umbrella-like steel branches. The Fujioka house of 1988 is typical of the series: at a considerable level of abstraction its interior seems a cousin to the trees seen through the glass beyond (figure 10).

So there is evidence that we like to have around us natural archetypes or simulations of them. But not all natural settings are places of tranquil reassurance. Literary portrayals of dense natural settings are often used to create anxiety in the reader; and there is real terror today in the thought of being left in the open on the African savanna that was our primary early home. We must have found or built, long ago, something other than trees and grasses, rivers and lakes; in whatever version of nature we found ourselves, we must have sought some more particular circumstances. What would they have been?

7
An outbuilding, the
Naiku site, Ise, 478(?).

8
Arne Bystrom,
the Connelly house,
Whidbey Island,
Washington, 1995
(© Arne Bystrom).

9
The chapter house,
Wells, 1250–1306.

10
Kazunari Sakamoto,
Fujioka house, Tokyo,
1988. The living room
(© Hiroyasu Fujioka).

The Refuge and the Prospect in Nature

One thing we need and have always needed is a place of protection. We need shelter from inanimate dangers: cold, rain, snow, sun; and we need concealment from hostile and dangerous animals, especially when we are particularly vulnerable. One such occasion is copulation. Our intuition to seek dark privacy for that activity is useful in a predator-laden world; concealment and darkness improve our chances of living to copulate another day. So "most human cultures demand that even socially condoned sexual behavior be carried on in private";[7] Shakespeare's "light and lust are enemies" and Sterne's "— Shut the door —" evidence sound observations about a survival-serving intuition. Similar intuitions explain our liking a place of concealment at times of sickness, sleep, childbirth, infancy, and childhood.

Among animals generally we humans especially need such a place for at least three reasons. The first is that as "feeble and almost defenseless primates,"[8] we lack many of the coping attributes other animals possess. Although I noted these in Chapter 1, they bear repeating: our teeth and claws are of limited effectiveness; we have no venom, no horns, no wings; we are neither very big nor very fast nor very well camouflaged; we have no shell or even a tough hide to protect against the teeth and claws of others; nor are our senses as acute as those of many other species. And we are poorly equipped to deal with the inanimate threats of climate: we have neither fur to protect against the cold nor adequate cooling systems to protect against the blazing sun. Finally, childhood, in which we depend on external support, is longer for us than for any other species except the elephant. It would have been essential from earliest times that we be programmed to find or create a haven for long-term concealment and protection against predation and weather.

The British geographer Jay Appleton has called this place of concealment and protection the *refuge*.[9] He considers the refuge concept to be of paramount importance, "one of the most fundamental in the symbolism of environmental perception. It finds extreme expression in the search for the nesting-place. If safety can't be secured, and if in consequence the individual organism ceases to function biologically, then all other desires become, for that individual, biologically irrelevant." Appleton illustrates the continuing presence of the refuge image in human awareness through numerous instances in poetry and painting. A poem by Sidney Lanier, "The Marshes of Glynn," describes the deep wood of

> Beautiful glooms, soft dusks in the noon-day fire, —
> Wildwood privacies, closets of lone desire,
> Chamber from chamber parted with wavering arras of leaves —.

Such settings—groves; or pocketed, contained spaces such as ravines; or in the extreme case caves, always in subdued light—such settings convey the possibility for hiding and therefore for safety. We seek them as we seek food and water.

But we must get food and water too, and in safety. We need access to a place where we can hunt and forage, a place that offers open views over long distances and is brightly lit, both to present a clear image of the landscape and to cast information-laden shadows—our fondness for sunlight may derive from its usefulness for this purpose. Such a place lets us hunt animals and gather plants while also revealing dangers that demand a retreat to the refuge. This more brightly lit open area of extensive views Appleton has named the *prospect*. Examples in poetry or painting are sunlit broad meadows or expanses of water. In Lanier's poem the poet moves from the refuge of "Wildwood privacies" to the prospect at the edge of the wood—"to the edge of the wood I am drawn, I am drawn," to "the vast sweet visage of space," a "world of marsh that borders a world of sea."

Refuge and prospect are opposites: refuge is small and dark; prospect is expansive and bright. It follows that they cannot coexist in the same space. They can occur contiguously, however, and must, because we need them both and we need them together. From the refuge we must be able to survey the prospect; from the prospect we must be able to retreat to the refuge. The eighteenth-century grotto at Stourhead garden, Wiltshire, with its meadow and lake (figure 11) is a concise artificial example of their immediate juxtaposition.

11
Henry Hoare,
the grotto,
Stourhead garden,
Wiltshire, 1740.
Micro-refuge and
manicured prospect.

12
W. Eugene Smith,
*The Walk to
Paradise Garden*
(© Kevin Smith).

Charles Dickens's *Bleak House* gives a tidy literary description of a largely natural prospect-refuge setting. Like Lanier, Dickens establishes his setting near the edge of a wood:

> We had one favourite spot, deep in moss and last year's leaves, where there were some felled trees from which the bark was all stripped off. Seated among these, we looked through a green vista supported by thousands of natural columns, the whitened stems of trees, upon a distant prospect made so radiant by its contrast with the shade in which we sat, and made so precious by the arched perspective through which we saw it, that it was like a glimpse of the better land.[10]

The requisite elements are all there: the sheltering grove whose subdued light and screen of "columns" keep the viewer unseen; the "arched perspective" to the "green vista," a "distant prospect made so radiant"; and finally the pleasurable human response to it all, "like a glimpse of the better land." Such a setting is captured by Eugene Smith's photograph *The Walk to Paradise Garden* (figure 12). (That those on Smith's "walk" are children constitutes a different and equally fundamental appeal, for like many species we are programmed to care for our young. Is it significant too that the children are boy and girl, that someday they will be capable of producing further offspring? The children's movement away from the camera implies the generational notion: they leave us behind, moving forward not only through space but also through time. The boy strides ahead, the first of the pair to advance from the hiding place into the meadow, and he looks to the right, the first movement in what we expect to be a scanning of the prospect ahead for advantages and dangers. The photo is a famous one and is available as a poster; people pay money to possess this image.)

The Refuge and the Prospect in Architecture

Dickens continues in the paragraph immediately following the one I quote above:

> The storm broke so suddenly—upon us, at least, in the sheltered spot—that before we reached the outskirts of the wood, the thunder and lightning were frequent, and the rain came plunging through the leaves, as if every drop were a great leaden bead. . . . As it was not a time for standing among trees, we ran out of the wood, . . . and made for a keeper's lodge which was close at hand. We had often noticed the dark beauty of this lodge standing in a deep twilight of trees, and how the ivy clustered over it, and how there was a steep hollow near, where we had once seen the keeper's dog dive down into the fern.

Dickens's characters look and move toward a building, which, like the grove they leave, offers a haven, but one of augmented security: it can provide not just concealment but also real protection against heat and cold, sun and (in this case) storm. In doing so it takes architecture back to its origins as an augmentation of refuge. "Buildings, as refuges, seem to offer not the fortuitous sanctuary of a cave or forest, but the planned sanctuary contrived with care and forethought for the express purpose of shielding vulnerable and sensitive man from the hostile forces to which he would otherwise be exposed."[11] And the lodge not only shelters Dickens's characters but also symbolizes its ability to do so before their practical need of it: embraced by a vestige of the grove (the "ivy clustered over it" and the "deep twilight of trees" in which it stands), its symbolism intensified by the "steep hollow near," it is a thing of "dark beauty." The Onrin-do illustrated in the Prologue (see figure 2) is another example of such a setting; so is the view within the Law Quadrangle at the University of Michigan (figure 13). Here too the building stands among trees. Its windows suggest places of concealment and elevated vantage point within, while the forms and patterns of the windows, and the "ivy clustered over," suggest that the building is analogous to, embraced by, its archetypal counterpart.

D. M. Woodcock has introduced a distinction between the characteristics of a setting we actually occupy and those of a setting we could occupy. He calls the conditions of an immediate setting *primary refuge* and *primary prospect*; conditions of a setting seen at a distance he terms *secondary refuge* and *secondary prospect*.[12] In this terminology the Stourhead grotto, Eugene Smith's photograph, and the first paragraph from Dickens are examples of primary

13
York and Sawyer,
The Law Quadrangle,
The University of
Michigan, Ann Arbor,
1923–33. The
northwest corner
of the court.

refuge and primary prospect: we occupy a refuge; from it we look toward a prospect. The view toward the Onrin-do in the Prologue and Dickens's lodge differ: in each of those cases we look toward a refuge but do not (yet) occupy it, nor do we view the prospects we expect will be available if we do occupy it. The Onrin-do and Dickens's lodge, then, in Woodcock's terminology, are secondary refuges, and the views we expect to see from them are secondary prospects. The view of the Michigan Law Quadrangle includes both primary and secondary conditions. The arcade at left and the rooms we imagine lying beyond the windows straight ahead are secondary refuges. The lawn, the walks, the flowers, as we imagine they might be seen from those secondary refuges, are a secondary prospect. But the tree trunk at right and the leaves at the top of the view locate us, at the moment of taking the picture, within a primary refuge of natural materials—from which the same lawn, walks, and flowers are a primary prospect.

Suppose we think of primary refuge in some purely architectural manifestation; what would that look like? The cloister at Salisbury (figure 14) is typical of a large family of examples. The columns, like Dickens's "natural columns," punctuate the view; the tracery above is similar in location and effect to the foliage of a grove; it filters the sunlight into dappled patterns as on a forest path. One looks outward to a Dickensian prospect that even to present-day eyes seems "like a glimpse of the better land." Alois Riegl in the nineteenth century observed that "the beginning of all artistic activity is the direct reproduction of natural objects aiming at the closest imitation possible."[13] But this cloister is not exactly that, nor is Riegl's statement the argument being made here. My point is not that this scene resembles nature in some "closest imitation" but that some architectural scenes and some natural ones accord—in form and space, in light and darkness—with an archetypal image whose physical manifestations would have conferred a survival advantage. Those of our species who long ago liked such a scene and were drawn to it would have had an unusually good setting for protection against threats and for exploitation of resources; so they would have maximized their chances for launching a genetically similar next generation. In this way an innate liking for such scenes would have persisted, even intensified, with the procession of generations over time and into the present. From this point of view Salisbury is an especially interesting example because the reason for its creation supports the point: this was never a monastic site; the cloister was built just because its characteristics were liked.

The Alhambra's Court of Lions is one the most evocative of such spaces. Its edges are arcades whose columns support spandrels cut through with ornamental pattern, filtering the sunlight like the foliage of a glade. From these arcades one looks outward to the sunlit meadow, where the animals are gathered around the water source (figure 15). Around and across the meadow are the secondary refuges of the far arcades; behind are even more secure refuges under the darker, denser foliage of the intimately detailed, softly lit interiors. Like Salisbury, the Alhambra is an especially appropriate example to cite. From one point of view it is a building with unusually specific meaning: it incorporates symbols and messages exclusively pertinent to Islam and its history.[14] Yet its appeal as an example of prospect-refuge juxtaposition depends, not on enculturation or cognitive content, but on universal and immediate emotional response. In this sense its appeal is not to the Muslim only but to Homo sapiens.

In the Salisbury cloister and the Court of Lions we stand roughly at the seam between refuge and prospect; our location in each case invokes the phrase in Lanier's poem: "To the edge of the wood I am drawn." The perceptions of the nineteenth-century poet and the intuitions of the medieval architect are supported by the laboratory work of the modern be-

14
Salisbury cathedral,
Wiltshire, 1220–1360.
The cloister.

15
The Alhambra,
Granada, 1333–54.
The Court of Lions
(© Cory Crocker).

havioral scientist: empirical studies by the psychologist Stephen Kaplan identify the "edge of the wood" as the place of innate human choice. "It becomes clear that neither being out in the open nor being in the woods is favored. These opposing vectors would tend to place the individual right at the forest edge. Ecologists point out that such an area is the richest in terms of life forms; it is likely to be the safest as well."[15]

16
Frank Lloyd Wright,
Taliesin, near Spring
Green, Wisconsin,
1911–59. From the
river, as it was
ca. 1959 (© Douglas
and Jennifer Varey).

The exterior features of a building can signal potential prospect and refuge. In the Michigan Law Quadrangle of figure 13 the arcade at left, the dark windows ahead surrounded by foliage, and the dark doorway suggest occupiable secondary refuges where one might see without being seen. A terrace, a secondary prospect–claiming platform, is evident forward of the chimneys at upper left. Appleton notes that "windows, alcoves, recesses, balconies, heavy overhanging eaves, all suggest a facility of penetration into the refuge." These and similar features can signal prospect as well. Horizontal expanses of opening suggest broad arcs of view; numerous and generous balconies and terraces imply commanding outlook over the terrain. Frank Lloyd Wright's houses present these characteristics consistently and profusely; Taliesin, his home in central Wisconsin of 1911–59, is typical (figure 16). Deep overhanging eaves, alcoves and recesses, the withdrawal of the house into the dense foliage, and the cave-like masses of stone anchoring the house to the hill all convey that this is a haven within which one can withdraw secure. Extensive bands of window and the balcony reaching out over the falling landscape, moreover, indicate that the advantages of generous prospect are likely to be available within.

The Pleasure of a Prospect to Water

If the camera had been moved back a few feet to record this view of Taliesin, the river that flows through the property would have been in the foreground; this river and a small lake fed by it are seen in considerable expanse from within the building. There is water in the Court of Lions too, and water appears in two of the illustrations of the Prologue. Water is not a universal feature of pleasurable settings, and of course it can suggest danger in certain instances. More often it augments a sense of comfort, especially when it is still or gently flowing, as in these examples.[16] So fountains and pools are frequent garden amenities for those who can have their way in such matters; and in areas where views to natural water features are available, buildings that offer such views command a substantial premium in the real estate market. The appeal of water in our surroundings can be explained in survival terms: drinking it at frequent intervals is essential to life. But its proximity has other advantages.

> There is considerable evidence from excavations in East Africa that even early hominids often located their camps at the edge of water. The survival-related advantages would have included immediate availability of drinking water, security and defense advantages, attraction of animals that could be hunted, and in some locations (seacoast, estuary, salmon river) extremely high food productivity associated with fish, shellfish, and crustaceans. Coss and Moore (1990) have argued that the capacity to find drinking water has acted as a major source of selection during evolution. Accordingly both modern children and adults evidence strong preferences for scenes with water.[17]

Thus water is often invoked in literature as a complement to refuge and prospect, as in Wordsworth's *Intimations of Immortality*:

> There was a time when meadow, grove, and stream,
> The earth, and every common sight,
> To me did seem
> Apparelled in celestial light,
> The glory and the freshness of a dream.

John Ruskin observes that "as far as I recollect, without a single exception, every Homeric landscape, intended to be beautiful, is composed of a fountain, a meadow, and a shady grove."[18] And Melville in *Moby Dick* describes a scene that recalls the first illustration of the Prologue:[19]

Here is an artist. He desires to paint you the dreamiest, shadiest, most enchanting bit of romantic landscape in all the valley of the Saco. What is the chief element he employs? There stand his trees, each with a hollow trunk, as if a hermit and a crucifix were within; and here sleeps his meadow, and there sleep his cattle; and up from yonder cottage goes a sleepy smoke. Deep into distant woodlands winds a mazy way, reaching to overlapping spurs of mountains bathed in their hill-side blue. But though the picture lies thus tranced, and though this pine-tree shakes down its sighs like leaves upon this shepherd's head, yet all were vain, unless the shepherd's eye were fixed upon the magic stream before him.[20]

Interior Refuge and Prospect

Jørn Utzon, winner of the Sydney Opera House competition in the late 1950s and a much-honored architect in his native Denmark, in the 1990s built two houses for himself on Majorca. The living room of Can Lis, circa 1990 (figure 17), opens to a magnificent view through splayed masonry-framed openings; these openings, when approached, provide a 180-degree view, through prismatic tunnels, of the land and sea beyond. A deep arc of seating is withdrawn into the pocket of opaque masonry walls opposite the view. The room suggests within itself two somewhat different zones: the withdrawn zone of the seating arc, and the more open and somewhat brighter zone forward of it. A large but simple stone-lintel fireplace marks the seam between the two zones. The spatial distinction is more clearly marked in the living room of Utzon's second Majorca house, of about 1995, Can Feliz (figure 18). This space contrasts a high and bright zone on the left toward the view with a low and dark zone to the right, the "low" in this case being achieved by raising the floor level. We could here begin to speak of refuge and prospect as concepts manifested entirely in a building's interior. Here, at right, an *interior refuge* has been developed by opaque walls, a lesser floor-to-ceiling dimension, and a low light level. Contiguously at left a complementary zone of *interior prospect* has been created by a somewhat greater floor-to-ceiling dimension, walls with extensive transparent surfaces, and a much higher light level.

In the Can Feliz living room the differences in light level and in distance from the actual exterior view distinguish the two zones. The plan dimensions of the two zones are similar, and the difference in ceiling height is modest. Interior refuge might be further augmented by opaque walls that establish much smaller horizontal dimensions and a ceiling plane that

17
Jørn Utzon, Can Lis,
Majorca, ca. 1990.
The living room
(© Arkitektens
Forlag/Søren Kuhn).

18
Jørn Utzon, Can Feliz,
Majorca, ca. 1995.
The living room
(© Arkitektens
Forlag/Søren Kuhn).

establishes a much smaller vertical dimension — and this last point deserves emphasis, for as Philip Thiel, Ean Duane Harrison, and Richard S. Alden have shown,[21] the ceiling plane is more important than any other in creating a sense of containment. Such internal refuge zones, as here, also depend on light levels significantly lower than those of surrounding areas. Thus windowless corner spaces, spaces closed on three sides, spaces of small dimension with low ceilings and prevalent solid walls announce themselves as protective retreats within the totality of an architectural interior. Halls and stairways, especially when narrow and low, bring wall and ceiling surfaces close to the body and so suggest protection and enclosure. There have been many iterations of interior refuge in architectural history: the inglenook, the den of the recent American home, the British snug or snuggery. The recurrence of such spaces may be its own argument that they deserve to be taken seriously.

Interior prospect depends on opposite characteristics: relatively generous plan dimensions, a significantly raised ceiling plane, significantly increased light levels, and generous expanses of transparent surface. When one space is significantly opened to another, the extended vista will contribute to a sense of interior prospect. Vistas through hallways that open to more distant windowed spaces conjoin interior and exterior prospect. The durably popular window seat provides interior prospect (the room that exists to one side), exterior prospect (the typically extensive outlook in the other direction), and the interior refuge of the window seat space itself.

Beatriz Colomina discusses such characteristics in several houses by the early-twentieth-century Viennese architect Adolph Loos and describes their experiential advantages. She says of a raised sitting area off the living room of the Moller house in Vienna of 1928: "The book shelves surrounding the sofa and the light coming from behind it suggest a comfortable nook for reading. But comfort in this space is more than just sensual, for there is also a psychological dimension. The position of the sofa, and its occupant against the light, produces a sense of security."[22] From this interior refuge both interior and exterior prospects open:

> Comfort in this space is related to both intimacy and the control of the scene. . . . A person inside the space can easily see anyone crossing the threshold of the house and monitor any movement in the interior. . . . The only exterior view that would be possible from this position requires that the gaze travel the whole depth of the house, from the alcove to the living room to the music room, which opens on to the back garden. Thus, the exterior view depends upon a view of the interior.

She notes of a similar raised sitting space at the center of the Müller house in Prague of 1930:

> Here, too, the most intimate room resembles a theater box, and overlooks the entrance to the
> communal area of the house, so that any intruder could easily be seen. . . . Suspended thus
> in the middle of the house, this space assumes a dual character: it has a "sacred" quality, but
> it is also a point of control. Paradoxically a sense of comfort is provided by two seemingly op-
> posing conditions, intimacy and control.

Similar observations can be made of Frank Lloyd Wright's houses. I have mentioned their
external characteristics (see figure 16); Nikolaus Pevsner notes that "the low spacious interiors [of those same houses] have something irresistibly inviting."[23] One reason for the irre-
sistible invitation may be that the promises of the exteriors are so richly kept in the interiors.
Few buildings have offered so consistently what I call a *nested hierarchy* of refuge and
prospect. The Edwin Cheney house in Oak Park, Illinois, of 1904 is typical (figure 19).
Wright's usual exterior features play their usual roles: alcoves, deep eaves, broad expanses of
window, and terraces and balconies suggest places of concealment and at the same time convey the availability of broad arcs of view over surrounding terrain. They tell us that the house
in its entirety is likely to be an effective refuge, and its interior is likely to offer unusually gen
erous prospect.

19
Frank Lloyd Wright,
the Edwin Cheney
house, Oak Park,
Illinois, 1904. From
the street, a drawing
by Marion Mahony.
(© University
of Washington
Photographic
Services.)

A convoluted path leads to an understated entry that, as it gives access to the interior, also emphasizes the refuge role of the house by shielding it from uninvited intrusion. Just inside the entry is the fireplace, with its implications of warmth and light (figure 20), under a low ceiling with opaque walls nearby to either side and the level of light low in comparison not only with that of the exterior but also with that of nearby interior spaces. This is an interior primary refuge, small, low, dark, warm, cozy. But we can choose between this and a quite different condition, for forward of the interior refuge the ceiling planes of the living room open into the volume of the roof and echo its geometry; hence they are much higher than the flat ceiling of the fireplace zone. These ceiling planes continue uninterrupted over the dining room to the north and the library to the south (figure 21), uniting the three spaces and inviting the eye to move from one to another; this is the spatial characteristic Wright called "the destruction of the box." And so the value of that "destruction": it provides contiguous interior prospect and refuge within a residential interior of modest size. Appleton notes: "If the eye makes a spontaneous assessment of the environment as a strategic theatre for survival, this must include some assessment of the opportunity for movement between the various key-positions in the prospect-refuge complex."[24] On the edges of the interior distant from the fire are expanses of glass with sweeping views (figures 19, 21) emphasizing exterior prospect to

20

Cheney house.
Interior refuge: the
low-ceilinged dark-
walled fireplace zone
of the living room.
Entry is to the right
of the fireplace
(© Christian Staub).

21

Cheney house. Interior
prospect: view from
the dining space with
the living space in the
middle ground and
interior refuge at its

left. The music room
terminates this interior
vista but windows
continue the view to
plantings beyond
(© Christian Staub).

the landscape; beyond is the generous terrace. Wright typically either lifted the main floor above grade, as here, or managed the plan so that main spaces overlook falling terrain, as at Taliesin (see figure 16). Either approach yields a commanding elevated view of an extended vista.

So the house in toto is refuge offering prospect; within are interior refuge and prospect. On the site of the house itself, beyond the architectural boundaries, we find that the duality occurs again. The drawing of the house (by Marion Mahony, who did most of Wright's presentation drawings at that time; see figure 19) is typical of the way Wright chose to have his houses portrayed.[25] It shows the building against an appealing background that was more than a convention of presentation; Wright meant to indicate how actual vegetation was to be located.[26] Refuge zones of the house would be withdrawn into the wood; prospect zones would reach forward into the meadow. Wright locates the inhabitant at "the edge of the wood" to which Sidney Lanier was drawn and where Dickens placed his characters—Kaplan's "forest edge" of innate human choice.[27]

22
Mario Botta,
house at Stabio,
Switzerland, 1980–81.
From the south
(© Mario Botta).

Wright's houses are remarkably consistent examples of a nested hierarchy of exterior and interior prospect and refuge features. But they are not the only examples, and the inclusion of these features does not depend on derivations of Wright's architectural vocabulary. In recent decades the Italo-Swiss architect Mario Botta has done many houses, on which much of his fame rests. These do not resemble Wright's in any obvious way, and no critic has linked the two; Botta's inspirations are, on the face of it, Le Corbusier, Palladio, and primarily the Estonian-American Louis Kahn, for whom Botta once worked. Nevertheless his spatial configurations are describable in the same terms as Wright's and are equally receptive to a prospect-and-refuge interpretation.

Botta's mature configuration appears in a house of 1980–81 at Stabio, Switzerland. On the exterior are alcoves, recesses, and large expanses of window (figure 22). There are no overhanging eaves in the usual sense, but windows are recessed so deeply into the volume of the building that the effect is the same: concealment is implicit in the recesses, while the over-

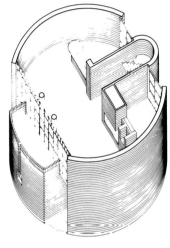
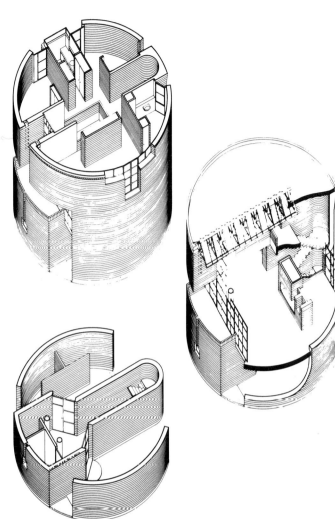

hanging brows suggest a panoramic outlook from within. From the entry vestibule, with ambiguous dual paths like those of the Cheney house, one doubles back up the towered stair to arrive on the main floor, near the fireplace and under a low ceiling (figures 23, 24). Behind is the masonry shell of the house, creating a pocket of space of which the fireplace is the focus. In the center of the house the volume extends dramatically upward and a glazed ceiling opens to the sky. Opposite the fireplace is extensive glazing whose doors lead to an elevated terrace looking over a gentle fall of land to a distant horizon (figure 25). Botta's house of 1982 at Viganello or that of 1984 at Bellinzona can be described in the same way.

24
House at Stabio.
Central atrium looking
toward the stair. The
fireplace of the living
space is at right, under
the low ceiling; the
dining space is at left
(© Mario Botta).

25
House at Stabio.
Central atrium looking
toward the terrace and
the landscape beyond.
The living space is at
left; the fireplace is
behind the camera at
left (© Mario Botta).

Wright's houses seem refuge-dominant; there is a paramount urge to snuggle up in spaces of peerless coziness. Botta's spaces seem roughly equally balanced between refuge and prospect. The work of Le Corbusier, in contrast, is often prospect-dominant. Each facade of the elevated main floor of his best-known house, the Villa Savoye at Poissy-sur-Seine of 1929 (figure 26), has either a window or a window-like opening across its entire extent, so a view is available in any direction. Interior spaces open to one another — the "plan libre." From the "salon" and the central circulation area — hallways, ramp, and stairs — other spaces are seen through layers of glazing in a way rarely achieved by Wright or Botta. Furthermore, though the house is painted in a number of bright colors, the dominant impression has always been of whiteness, so light reflectance is maximized throughout. There is little change in ceiling height from one space to another; all spaces are of relatively even light quantity; the living room fireplace is in front of an extensive window band with no surrounding architectural material to suggest a zone of containment (figure 27). So there are many prospects but few refuges. The Villa Savoye was a weekend house, and as such its dearth of refuge might be appropriate. Even so, one has to suppose that it could be happily occupied only by inhabitants unusually comfortable with a wealth of prospect and with minimal refuge needs. We do not know whether the Savoye family fit the description; they have left no record of their long term evaluation of the villa.

In another instance, however — a group of houses by Le Corbusier — there is tangible evidence of inhabitants' reactions: we know what changes they have made.

In 1920–21 Le Corbusier began a project for mass low-cost housing at Pessac, near Bordeaux. The construction of the houses took a long time, and they were not put up for sale until 1930, at which time about a hundred had been completed; no more were built. It is impossible to describe a single typical scheme because there were four types with varied site conditions. But all employed a "plan libre"; all had major spaces of unusually generous dimensions and a bath and kitchen of unusually meager dimensions. All employed Le Corbusier's "wide window" running the full width of the space served. All had flat roofs without overhangs and therefore without eaves. Many had terraces contiguous to a significant inhabited space but, oddly, seldom visible from that space. All had a roof terrace that was not contiguous to, or visible from, a major interior space and could be reached only by leaving that space and ascending a stair.

The houses remain — with changes. In his book of 1969, *Lived-in Architecture: Le Corbusier's Pessac Revisited*, Philippe Boudon detailed the ways in which the houses have been

26
Le Corbusier, the
Villa Savoye, Poissy-
sur-Siene, 1929.

27
The Villa Savoye.
The living space.

regarded and remodeled.[28] What changes have been most common? The wide windows of almost all examples have been reduced to more traditional widths, occasionally with shutters; there are a few added overhangs and a few awnings. These changes are consistent with refuge needs. An eave or overhang and smaller windows suggest that one can withdraw into the shadowed concealment of the house—not a message conveyed by the original wide un-shaded windows, from which one could see but behind which one could also be seen. In many cases at Pessac the large major rooms have been subdivided. This too suggests a need for refuge, although the suggestion rests on less certain ground since, as Boudon notes, the local tradition is one of smaller self-contained rooms.

Finally Boudon notes that the roof terraces have been little used and are even resented. In fact they are the focus of the most frequent complaint at Pessac, for interesting reasons:

> You know, it's almost a joke . . . nobody ever uses these terraces, except for the big buildings over there on the right, where the people use their big flat terrace, which is right at the top of the house, to hang out their washing . . . but nobody arranges flower-beds or puts out wrought iron tables and chairs like the people in Arago or Camponnac. And why? because they have loggias [in Arago] with direct access from the living room. So you can go straight from the living room to the terrace.[29]

Terraces enhance prospect in an obvious way: they offer extensive and panoramic views. Their symbolic value, however, may be more important than their actual use value: and if this is so, the terrace will be prized—whether used or not—only as long as it is visible from the refuge to complete the prospect and refuge duality. The frustration at Pessac arises from the existence of a terrace that is denied meaningful contiguous relationship to its complement. If Homo sapiens is programmed to respond positively to the prospect-refuge conjunction, do we feel resentment at the denial of expectation? An affirmative answer is admittedly speculative, but the quotation above vividly suggests it.

Boudon often mentions the tenants' interest in flowers and plants and illustrates how some terraces have been made into container gardens and how incongruous flower boxes have been added under windows. Photographs of the Villa Savoye taken over the years also often show the terrace as a container garden. These are additions. Typically in Le Corbusier's work the distinction between the fabricated and the natural is crisp and clear, and no provision is made for including plant material within the architectural fabric. In this respect (as of course in many others) Le Corbusier's work differs sharply from that of Wright. The interweaving of architecture with site and the specific provision for plant material in the architecture are hallmarks of Wright's work. Motifs deriving from plant forms are also often used in the architecture itself, as in the frieze of Hollyhock house, or the windows of the Ennis-Brown house (figure 28). It may be that part of Wright's lay appeal lies in this intimate relationship of architecture to natural materials—a primordial appeal on permanent loan, as it were. If so, such a relationship is likely to have a continued and predictable value, one based on more than mere romanticism.

Frank Lloyd Wright,
the Ennis-Brown
house, Los Angeles,
1923–24. A view
through the foliage
of a bower.

Prospect and Refuge in Other Building Types

Do such architectural characteristics belong only to detached low-rise dwellings? They occur occasionally, and might be made to occur more frequently, in the urban high-rise dwellings that clearly must be a major part of our future housing stock. The architect Gordon Walker included them in a condominium unit in Seattle of 1986. The entry (figure 29) is a tiny hallway whose short path turns, conveying an abbreviated sense of removal. Although the room that lies ahead is brighter and larger than the entry hall, its protective role is suggested by lower ceiling planes bounding the space on all sides (figure 30). Interior prospect is provided by opening sizable vistas from the living space to dining and study areas (figure 31). On the external wall an expanse of glass opens to a generous terrace, partly covered, partly not (figure 30). There is no extensive landscape beyond, but at least half the terrace is garden, so green and growing things occupy much of the cone of vision. This terrace is elevated very substantially over surrounding "terrain," and to the west the view includes the expanse of Elliott Bay. In a residence of only 850 square feet on the sixth floor of a twenty-story building, the degree to which prospect and refuge features have been provided offers hope for buildings similar in location, height, and purpose. Some features are more or less inevitable in such a building: the darker and lighter sides of the spaces, for example, arise from the plan imperative for a circulation core. But other features — manipulation of ceiling planes, provision for interior prospect, and a balcony or terrace partly covered, partly open to the sky — deserve design attention.

29
Gordon Walker,
a condominium unit,
the Watermark Tower,
Seattle, 1986. The
entry hall.

30
Watermark Tower
condominium. Looking
from the hall to the
living space, with
the terrace beyond.

31
Watermark Tower
condominium. Interior
prospect from the
living space to kitchen
and dining.

The prospect-refuge model is most obviously appropriate to the dwelling since it arises from those intuitions that long ago helped us to choose good dwellings. But it is appropriate to buildings other than the dwelling. Karl Friedrich Schinkel's Altes Museum in Berlin of 1822–30 is a radically different building type; from its upper lobby (figure 32), an elevated vantage point with its own column forest, one looks outward to the brighter, larger stair volume and thence to the Lustgarten beyond. The Seattle architectural offices of George Suyama, of 1997, include a similar arrangement of space and light for a different purpose and a different time. A small elevated withdrawing space is reached by an impressive run of stairs (figure 33). A strip of glass at floor level and a tiny oculus high in the rough concrete wall are the only sources of natural light for this tiny room, so although the floor is washed with light, the space itself is relatively dark (figure 34). Its only real view is past the pseudo-classical columns — architectural progeny of primordial groves — toward the much larger skylit display space at the foot of the stair; beyond are still brighter workspaces whose distant windows include a bit of natural material (figure 35). The project, which has received major professional

32
Karl Friedrich Schinkel, Altes Museum, Berlin, 1822–30. The view from the refuge of the upper lobby toward the brighter stairway and the Lustgarten beyond.

33
George Suyama, professional offices, George Suyama Architects, Seattle, 1997. The stair to the withdrawing space.

34
Suyama offices. The
withdrawing space.

35
Suyama offices.
The view from the
withdrawing space
through the trees
to meadows below
and beyond.

recognition,[30] was designed at the threshold of a new millennium; yet its relationships of space and light lie a hundred millennia deep in time. Graduate students at the University of Washington have also explored the value of a wide array of prospect and refuge choices in thesis projects for an AIDS hospice and a home for abused children, on the hypothesis that by such means some element of contentment might be brought into lives urgently in need of it.[31]

Prospect and Refuge: Caveats and Considerations

Individuals have been shown to vary widely in the balance they seek between the two extremes in the prospect-refuge juxtaposition. Where the configuration of a setting of long-term occupancy is at issue — remodeling an individual workplace, designing or buying or landscaping a home, arriving at the most appropriate spatial choices for a large office staff — one may want to consider the matter of preferences seriously and in detail. The prospect and refuge terms themselves assist discussion; having shown themselves to be easily understood without elaborate definition, they are useful for exchanges of individual feelings about the conditions they describe.

There seems to be a difference in emphasis between the sexes: women, on the whole, seem to prefer a balance weighted toward refuge, men toward prospect.[32] These preferences have appeared with remarkable consistency in several design studios with fifty-fifty gender distribution at the University of Washington; the sampling is small but the consistency is impressive. A similar preference has been found at a Seattle hotel lounge that has unusually clear refuge and prospect alternatives: women typically outnumber men in the interior refuge, while distribution in the interior prospect is usually roughly balanced. To test the point a little further, the psychologist Judi Heerwagen and the zoologist Gordon Orians examined landscape paintings by contemporaneous women and men from this point of view. They found that paintings by women are more refuge-dominant, and a majority of figures within them are refuge-located, while paintings by men show a similar bias toward prospect.

> Given substantial differences between the sexes with regard to reproduction and subsistence activities, males and females should use and assess environments differently. Although both males and females should find refuges attractive, for several reasons females should show a greater affinity for enclosure and protected places than do males . . . males should show greater affinity for open, prospect-dominant landscapes that in our evolutionary past sup-

ported the large game herds. . . . We tested the gender hypothesis by conducting a content analysis of male and female landscape paintings. . . . Almost half of the women's paintings had high refuge symbolism compared with only 25 percent of the men's paintings. . . . Thus, as expected, men did not reject refuge entirely but found it less compelling than did women. Also, as predicted, men's paintings were more concerned with prospects: almost half of their paintings were in the high prospect category compared to only a quarter of the women's paintings. . . . Women painters were more likely to place both male and female figures in refuge settings; . . . Men painters placed 62 percent of their male figures and 26 percent of their female figures in open spaces.[33]

Since few buildings are used exclusively by one sex or the other, these apparent gender differences suggest that any given setting ought to provide a range of choice of refuge and prospect conditions — and this issue deserves a little further discussion. There is a good bit of evidence to support what common sense would suggest: that individuals possess varying needs for each condition, and these varying needs relate not only to gender, as noted above, and to individual personality but also to time of day, time of year, and time of life. Thus the availability of a generous range of choice is likely to be of real value, yielding a malleable surrounding capable of accommodating changing moods and emotional needs. With a generous selection of alternatives, the occupant of an architectural setting can move to change the immediate condition from refuge, or a choice of diverse refuges, to prospect, or a choice of diverse prospects; and when the occupant's preferences change again, movement will satisfy again.

The examples discussed here suggest that we value indications of secondary refuges and prospects on the exterior of a building or building group. These include features to suggest penetrability into a zone of concealment and features to suggest that from within there is significant outlook. Thus the value of deeply shadowed voids that include apparent and generous areas of transparency. Terraces — architectural meadows — of generous size seem important whether frequently occupied or not; they gain in appeal if elevated above the scene they survey.

Interior prospect and refuge depend on a juxtaposition of significantly different spatial sizes and light conditions. These characteristics are not provided by the collection of rooms with similar plan dimensions, uniform ceiling height, and relatively uniform distribution of light. Interior prospect and interior refuge require a more complex and varied spatial com-

36
The Shisen-do,
Kyoto, 1636.

position, a requirement that especially suits them to our own time, with its remarkable possibilities for the free manipulation of space and light. Interior refuge is established on plan by opaque boundaries through something like two to three hundred degrees of perimeter arc that define spaces of relatively small plan dimensions. The sectional condition is even more important: interior refuge demands a ceiling palpably near the top of one's head. Vistas must be short, arcs of vision modest. But one view from the interior refuge is essential, and that is the view to an adjacent interior prospect. The interior prospect is opposite in every way: opaque wall surfaces, if any, must be at relatively much greater distances, the ceiling plane must be significantly higher, a broad arc of extended view must be offered. An exterior prospect-claiming platform, a terrace or balcony, should be visible and accessible. And these matters of vertical and horizontal largeness and smallness, view availability and view dimension are all closely related to the matter of light quantity.

I would emphasize the importance of light—and of darkness: the most difficult of architectural considerations.[34] They determine some of our most basic feelings of comfort and interest within settings. Contrast of light quantity has been a key element in valued architectural spaces over several millennia; it is essential to the prospect-refuge model. Through much of the twentieth century vast areas of glass have been typical of buildings large and small, with the assumed beneficial objective of admitting large and relatively uniformly distributed quantities of light. The energy crisis, with its restrictions on glass area, may make a positive contribution by encouraging us to consider that not all spaces should have high light values; some may be better relatively dark. Brilliant light — sunlight especially — reveals conditions in the prospect both by illumination and by the casting of shadows, which may go a long way toward explaining the value we place on sunshine. But we value the dark place of concealment too; that is where we procreate, and sleep, and meditate, and recover from illness and injury. It is our essential and reassuring haven in times of vulnerability. One thinks of Junichiro Tanizaki's *In Praise of Shadows*, and the dark recesses of the Japanese house, whose ambience he cherished (figure 36).[35]

Finally, the appeal of these characteristics arises in part from the requisites of aeons of survival in a predator-laden environment. In relatively recent times, evolutionarily speaking, most, but not all, land areas of the earth would have been predator-laden; therefore the appeal of the prospect-refuge juxtaposition may be argued for most, but not all, peoples. The most obvious exception of which I am aware is the Australian continent. It lacks a major land-based predator; and many contingents of the indigenous population seem not to have been programmed — selected — to choose a prospect-refuge habitat. Their dwellings can occur in the most exposed and seemingly vulnerable arrangements. I imagine there must be other similar instances. Nevertheless the appeal of prospect and refuge seems capable of illustration in a profusion of cultures across an impressive span of time.

37
The view from a side
street toward the
Palazzo Pubblico and
the Piazza del Campo,
Siena.

3

EXPLORING

THE VISTA ALONG THIS NARROW STREET in Siena is closed by brighter fragments of the buildings that stand at the edge of the Piazza del Campo (figure 37). The tower of the Palazzo Pubblico rises above the near cornices; the elaborate porch at its base is partly revealed, as are the windows and crenellated parapets of the palazzo; a few pedestrians wander along the street. Yet a lot is hidden—and it is immediately obvious to the eye that this is so. The near buildings intervene to hide what we expect to be more of the elaborate porch; details of the tower top are muted by mist; the ground plane appears to fall away in a downward slope, hiding its surface from our view. And the character of the light suggests—but only suggests—that an open expanse lies ahead to the right. If this view withholds so much of itself from us, why do we find it interesting? "Withholds" is the key: obviously a lot of information awaits discovery. The partly revealed, partly hidden fragments that close the vista urge exploration, which, we expect, will reveal more about the multiplicity of material that holds our attention

38
The view from a
side street toward the
cathedral, Orvieto.

and our interest. Hundreds of European towns offer variations on this scene; the vista toward the cathedral at nearby Orvieto (figure 38) is a famous example.

A similar exploratory urge is created by the approach to the shrine complex of Ryoan-ji (figure 39). The brightly lit body of material in view is obscured by the intervening foliage; it cannot be fully grasped from the vantage point shown. We feel compelled to find out more about whatever is partly revealed, partly hidden from us in such a view. Stephen Kaplan has empirically validated a preference for similar scenes in nature: "The most preferred scenes tended to be of two kinds. They either contained a trail that disappeared around a bend or they depicted a brightly lit clearing partially obscured from view by intervening foliage."[1] That last phrase, with its "brightly lit clearing" and "intervening foliage" is close to being a definition of prospect and refuge; for example, it fairly well describes the view to the Alhambra's Court of Lions if we accept the architectural material as intervening foliage. But Kaplan's definition differs in a subtle but important way, for in it he suggests that significant elements of the scene ahead are withheld from immediate view. This is true of the view of Ryoan-ji, and in this it differs from the view of the Court of Lions. The vista in Siena mani-

39
The approach to
the Ryoan-ji shrine,
Kyoto.

fests in a cityscape Kaplan's first setting, "a trail that disappeared around a bend." In each case there is the "promise that more information could be gained by moving deeper into the depicted setting." Kaplan proposes the term "mystery" for this characteristic.[2]

> Mystery involves not the *presence* of new information, but its promise. Mystery embodies the attraction of the bend in the road, the view partially obscured by foliage, the temptation to follow the path "just a little farther." While the "promise of more information" captures the essential flavor of this concept, there is actually more to it than that.
>
> Scenes high in mystery are characterized by continuity; there is a connection between what is seen and what is anticipated. While there is indeed the suggestion of new information, the character of that new information is implied by the available information. Not only is the degree of novelty limited in this way, but there is a sense of control, a sense that the rate of exposure to novelty is at the discretion of the viewer. A scene high in mystery is one in which one could learn more if one were to proceed farther into the scene. Thus one's rate and direction of travel would serve to limit the rate at which new information must be dealt with. For a creature readily bored with the familiar and yet fearful of the strange, such an arrangement must be close to ideal.
>
> Mystery arouses curiosity. What it evokes is not a blank state of mind but a mind focused on a variety of possibilities, of hypotheses of what might be coming next. It may be the very opportunity to anticipate several possible alternatives that makes mystery so fascinating and profound.[3]

Exploring mysteries has evolutionary benefit. "Curiosity does, we are told, sometimes kill cats. Nonetheless we believe that cats lacking curiosity fail to learn enough about their environments to function in them as well as their more curious brethren, even though being curious sometimes has its unfortunate consequences."[4] There may be delight or danger or both in the suggested but unseen environment. Exploration may reveal the presence or absence of suitable habitation, food, water — and also of threats to the creature. Its chances of survival are improved if it is — we are — intuitively driven to obtain this knowledge in relative safety. The stimulus is the suggestion but not the immediate revelation of an accessible environment. The response is exploration to obtain knowledge or information about that environment. Our information-seeking intuition is brought into play; it is driven and rewarded by the pleasure we find in exercising it.

(This pleasure in knowledge for its own sake is amazingly strong. We spend enormous amounts of money to investigate the "big bang"; to unearth Troy; to explore the moon; to find the *Titanic*, and make, and see, movies that show us what it was like; to describe dinosaurs with greater accuracy, and make, and see, movies that show us what *they* were like. All of these things interest us enormously; none have any direct pragmatic value. That new architectural information yields a related pleasure is attested by an owner of a Frank Lloyd Wright house, Samuel Freeman, who once said he had lived in the house for forty years and each morning discovered something new. The architect Eric Owen Moss makes a similar comment about a recent house of his design: "This is the hedonism of the space, loaded with new prospects one doesn't recognize, so that each time you come into the space you could say, 'I've never been here before.'"[5] Freeman and Moss obviously believe this continuing discovery is pleasurable. But there is no intrinsic reason why it should be, other than as the offering of novel information to a creature with a voracious appetite for it. This does not mean that our drive to seek knowledge has been useless to our evolution; on the contrary it is beyond doubt one of the key factors, perhaps *the* key factor, in our evolutionary success. But that behavior, like other innate behaviors, is not driven by thoughts of its pragmatic usefulness, and exists quite apart from any direct relationship to pragmatic usefulness.)

Kaplan notes a "brightly lit clearing" but not a brightly lit trail. In fact moving toward the light is important to either scene: if progress along the path is from darker to lighter, we will again be able to see without being seen, and so will ensure for ourselves relative safety during exploration. (The reverse, a path moving from light to dark, means that as one moves deeper into the space, one is seen without seeing. That is not so pleasant. Our aversion to that kind of mystery is sufficiently predictable that a path leading toward a partly revealed space, and leading from light to dark—"the dark at the top of the stairs"—is a staple of horror movies.)

I want to emphasize this matter of light in what Kaplan calls mystery, the positive value of mystery when accompanied by the opportunity to move toward a greater quantity of light. I suggest the term *enticement*, which might be defined as a view and opportunity for movement from one space to another whose features are only partly revealed, the occupied space being relatively darker and the partly revealed distant space relatively brighter. Enticement is like refuge and prospect in deploying light in a way that suggests safety, but it differs in concealing significant elements of what lies ahead.

The Enticing Setting

Significant elements of Ryoan-ji in its "brightly lit clearing" are "partially obscured from view by intervening foliage." The column forest and the complex superstructure of the Great Mosque at Cordoba serve too as intervening foliage (figure 40), partially obscuring from view rich information ahead in a brightly lit clearing. Exploratory intuitions urge us toward the

40
The Great Mosque,
Cordoba, 785–961.
The column forest
(© Cory Crocker).

41
The Great Mosque.
Near the mihrab
(© Cory Crocker).

light; our reward is the informational richness of the mihrab (figure 41).[6] The history of this building offers documentation of its cross-cultural appeal: Charles V of Spain so valued this space that he was outraged on learning of the insertion of a Christian cathedral into the column forest. The sanctuary of the cathedral of Saint Louis uses the same devices as at Ryoan-ji to invite exploration (figure 42).

The view along the tiny hallway of one of Frank Lloyd Wright's later houses, in contrast, presents to the eye an architectural "trail that disappears around a bend" (figure 43). Wright often used this device in his late small houses. It invites exploration that reveals new information with every step, creating in turn a sense of extended experience, hence of extended space (figure 44). The means are counterintuitive: one would think that terminating the vista in glazing would be the way to achieve the effect. But this approach works. Wright's Hanna house of 1936 in Palo Alto takes it a good bit further: its spaces constitute an architectural trail that *repeatedly* disappears around a bend (figure 45). The plan is based on a grid of regular hexagons, each corner of which describes an angle of 120 degrees; the spaces of the house repeatedly interconnect at this obtuse angle. So the spaces deflect but do not terminate;

42
Barnett, Haynes, and
Barnett, the Roman
Catholic Cathedral
of Saint Louis, Saint
Louis, Missouri, 1906–
88. The sanctuary as
seen from a side aisle.

43
Frank Lloyd Wright, a
small house of 1952–
57. The corridor vista.

44
Wright, a small house of 1952–57. The living room, with terrace at left.

45
Wright, the Hanna house, Palo Alto, 1936. The living space (© Ezra Stoller/Esto Photographics).

interior vistas are sweeps of bending space; distant material continually promises and continually provides additional information. And we always move toward the light because on the flank there is continuous dappled light from the glazed, finely mullioned walls. The Hanna house thus includes both enticement conditions: the architectural space is a trail that repeatedly disappears around a bend, while the mullions of the windows are intervening foliage through which the sunlit natural material is seen beyond. The enticements combine with Wright's usual multiple refuges and prospects to make spaces of magical interest and warmth.

The stair in the north transept of Wells cathedral manages to provide three enticements (figure 46). The bright space in the distance is the Chain Gate Bridge crossing a major street to a housing project constructed circa 1460; the room that is this bridge is partly masked by columns and superstructure; "a brightly lit clearing partially obscured from view by intervening foliage." The nearer part of the stair, from about 1290, is lit principally and of necessity from the windows at left. These face west, and late in the day they flood the space with directional light. By accident or design each further ascending riser of the arcing portion of the stair receives this light more directly, therefore reflects it more brightly. We are drawn toward the light and toward another partly revealed space, since it is increasingly apparent as we ascend that there is a second source of light drifting through the tracery at the top of the arc of stair (figure 47). So we are led along the "trail that disappears around a bend" to a third enticement, another "clearing obscured by foliage" (figure 48), the chapter house, an architectural grove with windows of arboreal tracery—Wordsworth's "imperial palace whence we came." Our early ancestors, who liked such a sequence of spaces, light, and pattern, were led to explore and discover and thereby obtained advantages that gave them better odds of launching successive successful generations. We, heirs to their intuitions, like the sequence too.

(Most observers also note with interest and pleasure the depressions worn into the steps by centuries of use. Do they tell us this path is safe; many of our species have traveled here; all will be well? And if so, is the message understood intuitively or cognitively? Among John Ruskin's *Seven Lamps of Architecture* is the "lamp" of Memory, within which he included such visible records of human use. His point may have a solid rationale.)

There are other comparable enticing stairways. A particularly elegant example is that of the Palazzo Carignano in Turin, of 1679–83, by Guarino Guarini, in which an enticing bright zone of half-hidden information occurs at the landing, and again at the top. Another

46
Wells cathedral,
Somerset. The Chain
Gate Stair from
the north transept,
1290–1460
(© Woodmansterne).

47
Wells. The tracery
at the top of the
arc of stair, with
the chapter house
coming into view.

48
Wells. The chapter
house grove seen
through the tracery.

49
The Palace of Minos,
Knossos. The stair in
the domestic quarter
of the palace.

50
The Palace of Minos.
A room with balcony on
the flank of the stair.

remarkable enticement stairway belongs to one of the earliest grand dwellings of which we
have record: the Palace of Minos from about 1600 B.C. near the modern village of Knossos on
Crete. The Grand Staircase of the palace originally linked four floors of the domestic quarter. (The stair is now as Arthur Evans reconstructed it early in the twentieth century. But
Evans rebuilt only the bottom two floors; the following discussion imagines the characteristics of the restored portion continuing through the original four stories.)[7] The stair is a series
of switchbacks along the flank of a light shaft open to the sky (figure 49). Light pours down
from above, so on the flank above is brightness. The light shaft also illuminates the floor itself, so on the flank below is brightness. We are never far from refuge since a retreat to the
withdrawn side of the stair brings the concealment of darkness and the reassurance of en-
closing surfaces; yet whether we move up or down, we move within these shaded stair runs
toward a brighter destination. The prospect across stair and light shaft seems absurdly short;
yet with movement up or down other volumes are sequentially hidden and revealed — rooms,
almost balconies, front on the shaft of light (figure 50) and as seen from the stair release a series of longer vistas. The new information they sequentially reveal adds to the stair's own invitation to explore.

Enticement can also occur through orthogonal interposition of parallel planes, much as a
sequence of theater stage flats might indicate unseen spaces extending laterally. This condi-

51

William Rimmer, *Flight
and Pursuit* (Bequest
of Miss Edith Nichols,
courtesy, Museum of
Fine Arts, Boston).

52

Carlo Scarpa,
Castelvecchio
Museum, Verona,
1972–75.

tion is part of the strangely arresting appeal of William Rimmer's painting *Flight and Pursuit* (figure 51); its architectural counterpart is Carlo Scarpa's Castelvecchio Museum in Verona of 1972–75 (figure 52), whose partly revealed gallery spaces extend laterally from the vista framed by the sequence of arches.

Some Special Cases of Enticement

There are buildings too in which simple darkness is the interposition between eye and information. I am thinking here of the family of buildings epitomized by the Cathedral of Notre-Dame-de-Chartres, considered by many to be an exceptionally moving and memorable architectural space. Surely those who feel this building's appeal would agree that the unusual darkness has something to do with it. The darkness withholds information, yet the light is just sufficient to suggest that a closer approach to any of the surfaces defining the space will offer greater information (figure 53). But where in the space is the information most dense? In the sources of light themselves, the windows. These we can approach — it is impossible to move in any direction without doing so — and in doing so we move, of course, always toward the light. But we remain, nevertheless, in relative darkness ourselves, since the windows, deepening the light in any case, are high above us, the brightest of them far away indeed. So although we can — must — always move toward the light if we move at all, nevertheless in this space, unlike the typical enticement setting, we can never move entirely into the light. (I am aware that these phrases may be read as metaphors of Christian theology, Christ or the Christian heaven being the light, and that such an interpretation may have been understood, consciously or subconsciously, at the time the cathedral was built.)[8] So in the vast space one can remain hidden—in no building of essentially one room is it easier to lose oneself—and one sees, though admittedly not clearly, without being seen. Yet one perceives everywhere the complex abundance of information: the sculptural and architectural complexities have stimulated centuries of study, and questions still remain. One moves and seeks, drawn by the light of the windows' complex brilliance, yet never fully arrives. The windows entice but remain out of reach; the seeking is continually reinforced, never completed. Why is this not frustrating? Because although we never close with it all—something is always withheld—exploration is always rewarded; more is always discovered.[9]

53
Chartres cathedral,
1194 – ca. 1225.
The windows of the
chevet seen from
the side aisle.

Atmosphere can function similarly to withhold information; this is the magic of settings experienced in thick weather, like the Kasuga shrine in Nara on a day of heavy rain (figure 54). With each step on such a day, at such a site, new material is revealed through exploration.

There is another possible permutation of the enticement experience. Walking east at the southeastern edge of Eliel Saarinen's Cranbrook Academy in Michigan of the 1920s, one approaches a vaulted passageway through which, beyond a small Carl Milles sculpture, a dense wood is seen (figure 55). Late in the day especially this wood glows with afternoon sun. We are drawn toward the light and so are induced to enter the passageway; as we approach the small sculpture, more of the sunlit wood is revealed (figure 56). At the midpoint of this passageway, however, still only the upper portion of the wood is seen; the ground plane appears only as we reach the passageway's end. So there is a clue that the passageway is well above the ground plane that belongs to the wood. The suggestion that the view will be toward a lower meadow reinforces our willingness to proceed, since the terminus is obviously going to be an elevated vantage point. At the end of the passageway views open not just to the woods but also to left and right. The one to the right is unremarkable, but at left an unanticipated vista opens (figure 57): cascades and reflecting pools, populated by anthropomorphic bits of bronze, lead

55
Eliel Saarinen
and Carl Milles,
Cranbrook Academy,
Bloomfield Hills,
Michigan, 1922–50.
A view to an arched
passageway.

56
Cranbrook.
In the passageway.

57
Cranbrook. The
cascade, library, and
museum (with Eero
Saarinen) as seen from
the landing at the end
of the passageway.

58
Saint-Trophime, Arles,
ca. 1150. Cloister
(© Jack O'Connell).

59
Palace of the
Normans, Palermo,
twelfth century.
A stair and courtyard
(© Joan Nilsson).

the eye to the animal-and-human piece at the end—Europa and the Bull—behind which is the propylaea of museum and library, the whole flanked by an extension of the wood first viewed. Unlike the previous enticements, at Cranbrook the information revealed by exploration is not what was suggested at the outset.

Enticement: Caveats and Considerations

Enticement reveals, but only partly reveals, an information-laden scene; discovery of further features depends on exploration, and such exploration must be encouraged by other supportive characteristics of the setting.

The concealed aspects may be hidden by solid opaque material, as at Siena or Orvieto or Cranbrook; or by intermittent screening elements, as at Wells or Ryoan-ji; or by both, as at the Hanna house; or by darkness, as at Chartres. But in all cases there must be the suggestion that the concealed material is interesting enough to make exploration worthwhile. The view from the cloister of Salisbury—that at Arles (figure 58) may be a better example—provides information sufficiently complete so that there is no particular urge to explore, whereas Siena or Chartres gives the immediate impression that a large amount of intriguing material awaits discovery. Exploration may disappoint, of course—what we see from the first vantage point may be all there is—though that is not the case in the examples cited. Enticement, then, depends on the presence of clues that significant interesting material remains to be discovered. This of course is a judgment call; what are adequate clues for some may be inadequate for others. The view from the stair of the Palace of the Normans at Palermo (figure 59) seems to me to lie on the borderline. Some may feel content with the information already on view and feel no urge to further discovery; others may be impelled to explore. The observer decides. In cases where the interposition of solid opaque material masks information, it seems important that the observer obtain further information by moving from relative darkness to relative brightness. In such a movement, we approach a space whose features are visible to us before we are visible to any creature within that space. In this respect enticement is similar to refuge and prospect: we see without being seen as we explore. The point needs emphasis because a reversal—pathway bright, terminal space dark—changes the response from enticement to anxiety. This is an issue of some importance in architectural interiors, and more so in the urban scene, where the dangers may be real and our intuitive refusal to explore may be quite immediately survival-advantageous.

If enticement demands movement from dark to light, how can there be a reversal of the path through the spatial sequence, as most architectural configurations require at some point? There may be a brightly lit zone of enticement at another terminus, or several, so the sequence includes multiple enticements; this is a sound strategy that can yield wonderfully rich spatial sequences. But the question also focuses on the spatial and formal characteristics of the darker path that links such a sequence of bright spaces. That path must be fairly free of places where danger might be concealed; no alcoves, no corners. This is true of the examples shown here—the streets in Siena and Orvieto, the stair at Wells, and the passageway at Cranbrook; each is free of places where danger might be imagined to lurk, so each entices without anxiety. If places of potential concealment do occur on such paths they must be relatively well lit so they too are prospect spaces—so that as we move toward and along them, we see without being seen.

Testing Our Exploratory Limits: The Thrill of Peril

A postcard popular in the English Lake District shows two people perched atop the pinnacle known as the Napes Needle (figure 60). Why is the postcard popular? Why are the people there? There is no reason to suppose any practical purpose to either the postcard or the perch, nor any reason to imagine that either postcard buyers or climbers have been coerced. So there must be something pleasurable in this for all parties. But what is it that is pleasurable? The prospect is extraordinary; no doubt of that. But the setting is obviously fraught with extreme danger: one slip and life is over. And we know that that is part of the point, that what the climbers, and the postcard buyers too, have sought and presumably are enjoying is the thrill of the place—and the word "thrill" is the key. It is a paradoxical word: it involves two emotions, fear and pleasure, that are normally mutually exclusive. In this setting and all voluntarily experienced settings that carry a similar component of danger, thrill is the emotion we seek and enjoy.

Appleton defines a number of conditions that give rise to the emotion of thrill; he groups these under the general heading of *hazards*.[10] I am going to reduce Appleton's list somewhat, and am going to propose the term "peril" for that reduced list—but let me first note Appleton's definitions. He groups hazards under three main headings: incident, impediment, and deficiency. Under incident hazards Appleton has two major subheadings, animate and inanimate. Within the animate, in turn, he cites human and nonhuman hazards. Although security against nonhuman predation was beyond doubt a primary early function of the refuge, this in any literal sense can be ignored for our purposes since in modern life we rarely confront it. Human hazards consist of unwanted human intrusions of whatever form; against these the refuge has also always played a protective role. Appleton's second category of inci-

60
The Napes Needle.

dent hazards, the inanimate, is a large group, the largest of his listings in fact; it comprises meteorological, instability, aquatic, fire, and locomotion hazards. The meteorological hazards include threats of climate: heat, cold, wind, sun, rain, and snow. Instability hazards are earthquakes, landslides, and avalanches; fire is self-evident.

Why do these arouse our interest? They intensify the value of the refuge by giving evidence of what it protects against; the haven becomes more dramatically a haven. Thus the contentment in being tucked safe in bed with rain pounding on the roof, or gathering around a fire with a storm raging outside; in each case security is dramatized by the nearness of discomfort and even danger. Melville writes to this point in *Moby Dick*:

> We felt very nice and snug, the more so since it was so chilly out of doors; indeed out of bedclothes too, seeing that there was no fire in the room. The more so, I say, because truly to enjoy bodily warmth, some small part of you must be cold, for there is no quality in this world that is not what it is merely by contrast. Nothing exists in itself. If you flatter yourself that you are all over comfortable, and have been so a long time, then you cannot be said to be comfortable any more. But if, like Queequeg and me in the bed, the tip of your nose or the crown of your head be slightly chilled, why then, indeed, in the general consciousness you feel most delightfully and unmistakably warm. . . . Then there you lie like the one warm spark in the heart of an arctic crystal.[11]

There is also a deeper reason. Appleton argues that survival requires sensitivity to danger signals, and this argument again invokes the pleasure-response rationale: "If we were to be interested only in those features of our environment which are suggestive of safety, cosiness and comfort, and not at all concerned with those which suggest danger, what sort of recipe for survival would that be? Seeking the assurance that we can handle danger by actually experiencing it is therefore itself a source of pleasure."[12]

The Always-Visible Hazard: Peril

All the hazards just noted are occasional and transitory; none of them is on permanent display; in the normal course of events no trace of them impinges on our senses. They constitute the entirety of Appleton's category of incident hazards, with two important exceptions: aquatic hazards and those of locomotion. Both differ from those already mentioned in having a continuous tangible and apparent presence. Of the aquatic Appleton says:

Even calm water can be a fatal hazard to a victim who cannot swim, but the destructive potential of water is more eloquently expressed when it is moving, and waterfalls, rapids, and storm waves figure consistently in the landscape furniture of the Sublime. Falling water can symbolize the power of the forces of nature whether in Niagara or in the absurdly genteel "cascade" of the eighteenth-century landscape gardeners.[13]

And of the hazards of locomotion:

One of the most prevalent is that of falling. We all know that fatal falls can be sustained even on level surfaces, but generally serious falls are associated with high elevations, and it is these which have the power of suggesting danger and arousing fear for those who encounter them. Here again, those landscape features which display this property, "beetling cliffs," chasms, precipices of all sorts, are among the hallmarks of the Sublime.[14]

Appleton calls these incident hazards. He lists a smaller category of impediment hazards, the most important of which, for our purposes, are also tangibly apparent:

In nature dense vegetation, cliffs, ravines, etc., may impede movement, as also may water-bodies of all sorts. . . . Rivers play a particular role in this respect, because under normal conditions they continue as lines of physical separation over long distances. . . . particular significance attaches to those places where such a hazard is terminated or interrupted. A crossing-place of a river, for instance, by a bridge or a ford, focuses the attention on the opportunity which it presents for circumventing or surmounting the hazard.[15]

These aquatic, locomotion, and impediment hazards, permanently on view in a setting, are the ones most directly important to the architectural experience. I suggest for these the term *peril.*

Peril as defined here differs from the anxiety of the previous chapter. Situations that breed anxiety may (or may not) hide dangers whose avoidance is not entirely within our control. Hence our response is one of fear unalloyed with pleasure. I cited in particular a reversal of light and darkness in what is otherwise a condition of enticement—an unseen darker space, perhaps with dangers, perhaps not, lurks beyond the better-lit viewpoint. Settings of peril, in contrast, comprise real dangers, seen or sensed, no question at all that they exist—but avoidance of them rests within our control, even if only by the exercise of considerable care and skill. This element of control in the face of danger creates the response of thrill. From

61
Frank Lloyd Wright,
Fallingwater, the
Edgar Kaufmann
house, Bear Run,
Pennsylvania, 1936.
Refuges and
prospects, ravine and
waterfall (Collection
John Savo).

it comes much of the appeal of such purely natural settings as Niagara Falls, the Grand Canyon, and the Matterhorn, all of which present dramatically visible hazards of locomotion; their precipices clearly announce the possibility of a fatal fall. At Niagara this announcement is enormously augmented by the "falling water," an aquatic hazard of unique drama. Such settings present dramatic, apparent, but manageable peril, confrontation with which brings thrilling elation.

The Unique Epitome of Perilous Architecture

Fallingwater, Frank Lloyd Wright's country house for the Kaufmann family in rural southwestern Pennsylvania, of 1936, is a rare instance of an architect's exploitation of peril in domestic design. To reach the house, one pushes through dense vegetation at the edges of a steep ravine and traverses a bridge across a tumbling river, all the while approaching the architectural beetling cliffs of the house. Yet on arrival the house is seen to have an abundance of refuge and prospect symbols. It has a profusion of deep overhanging eaves, windows, alcoves, and recesses that suggest penetrability and protection, a suggestion reiterated by the stone pylons that create cave-like rooms embedded in the geology of the site. The house also has a profusion of conspicuous and generous balconies to suggest sweeping outlook; they project east and west from the south edge of the living room and, even more dramatically, south from the main bedroom upstairs (figure 61). But all this refuge and prospect seems, and is, dangerously poised over danger. The balconies reach out into space, and because of prior knowledge, but also because their hovering character is recalled by the similar forms all around, there is the perceived danger of falling—and below is the ravine and the falls itself, heard even when not seen (figure 62). So the prospect-claiming terraces, with refuge behind, are also perilous precipices over space and over the falling water and the rapids. The concrete trays match and complement the peril of the site, and both trays and site intensify the refuge and prospect messages of the house itself. The paradoxical genius of this house, and perhaps the basis for its extraordinary fame and popularity, is that it dramatizes the peril of its setting and itself while insisting with unparalleled intensity that it is a haven of safety.

Fallingwater is an ideal example of the possibilities for exploiting peril as an architectural enrichment. But it depends on site conditions so rare that the suggestions it offers are of limited applicability; it has been and is likely to remain a unique instance of the broad range of attributes it presents. Even so, a roughly similar sense of haven in the face of discomfort and even danger is typical of much of Wright's work. One person who grew up in one of the best

62
Fallingwater.
A haven of safety
complementing
the peril of its
site and itself
(© Balthazar Korab).

63
Frank Lloyd Wright,
the Melvyn Maxwell
Smith house,
Bloomfield Hills,
Michigan, 1946. Snow
and storm, and the
participating refuge
(© Balthazar Korab).

of Wright's late houses, a cousin to that shown in figure 63, has left a comment strikingly similar to the earlier quotation from Melville: "It's really an exciting place to be in the middle of a blizzard when the snow was falling all around and we were inside. And there was a lot of fire warmth, heat, light and that huge fireplace, you know, but there was so much glass that we could be part of the, we could enjoy the snow and the storm outside, while still feeling safe inside." [16]

Peril as a Function of Height

One of the most wonderful and least discussed characteristics of the Athenian Acropolis is the surprise of its exhilarating height, the elation of its elevation above even the multistoried present-day city far below (figure 64). Such sites—we might call them buildable versions of the Napes Needle—often attract architectural efforts of one sort or another by virtue of their height alone.

In the Christian world a number of religious buildings put up centuries ago were located on similarly elevated sites for obvious reasons of safety: they had the fighting advantage of high ground and the reconnaissance advantage of prospect. We cannot know whether the thrill was an additional attraction to the original builders, but to modern visitors at sites such as the medieval monasteries of Meteora (figure 65) it is now the most striking and indelible impression. This sort of topography was often picked for sites dedicated to Saint Michael—Skellig Michael off western Ireland is an example, or the twelfth-century Chapel of Saint-Michel-du-Puy (figure 66). The best-known and most often visited of these is Mont-Saint-Michel off the Normandy coast. The town's narrow streets and the solidity of their surfaces suggest refuge; the shelter they offer from the sea is palpable; and they lead to the further

64
The Acropolis, Athens.
The western bastion,
with the temple to
Athena Nike above.

refuges of the ubiquitous hotels and, at the crown of the *mont*, the dark volume of the abbey itself. The hotels and the parvis of the abbey offer dramatic prospects to the sea; these also open from several points along the public open spaces (figure 67). Such viewpoints are architectural precipices from which a fall would be fatal; the thrill of occupying such a position can be felt even in the photograph. Henry Adams long ago understood this aspect of Mont-Saint-Michel:

> The Archangel loved heights. . . . His place was where the danger was the greatest; therefore you find him here. . . . So he stood for centuries on his Mount in Peril of the Sea, watching across the tremor of the immense ocean, — *immensi tremor oceani* — . . . . The church stands high on the summit of this granite rock, and on its west front is the platform, to which the tourist ought first to climb. From the edge of this platform, the eye plunges down, two hundred and thirty-five feet, to the wide sands or the wider ocean, as the tides recede or advance, under an infinite sky, over a restless sea.[17]

(Adams here suggests another characteristic of Mont-Saint-Michel, and the thrill that results from it, in the realm of the cognitive. Most visitors know from guidebooks or prior experience

65

Meteora.

66

Saint-Michel-du-Puy.

67
Mont-Saint-Michel.

that flood tides approach the *mont* with terrific speed; at high tide the causeway is submerged and the *mont* is cut off from the land; it becomes for a time an island. At this time, like most islands, it cannot be reached by land transport, but unlike most islands, it cannot be reached by boat either because the waters over the sands are shallow and will withdraw with the ebb. When the tide is in and one is not on the *mont*, one cannot get to it, and when one is on it, one cannot get off; movements usually taken for granted are here regularly suspended. We are controlled by rhythms of nature manifested in nature's hazard symbol, water; its presence commands our affective attention; its particular peril we know from cognitive awareness.)

The towers of Notre-Dame-de-Laon are architectural Napes Needles. The cathedral sits on the crown of a mesa in the Champagne; the mesa must be ascended before the further climb up the towers (figure 68). The elation of elevation is intensified by the architectural character. The French Gothic of the late twelfth and early thirteenth centuries, to which

68
Laon cathedral, 1155–
1215. The west towers
from the south
transept tower
(© Jack O'Connell).

these towers belong, attempted the ultimate reduction of solid material to create a cage or skeleton of stone. The remarkable towers of Laon are delicate to the point of apparent insubstantiality. We wonder, as the medieval mason must have wondered, whether the armature will stand, whether the shafts will hold even the modest added load of our own weight. These towers are perilously delicate mountaintops on a mountaintop, and are felt to be so. Few medieval cathedrals have a site like Laon — only English Durham and Lincoln come to mind — but all share the ambition for thrilling height. At Chartres Henry Adams felt "the peril of the heavy tower, of the restless vault, of the vagrant buttress" that led to the sensation of an "equilibrium . . . visibly delicate beyond the line of safety; danger lurks in every stone" (figure 69).[18]

Some buildings have been put up specifically to stimulate such sensations. The Eiffel Tower immediately comes to mind, a vast iron armature built to demonstrate French tech-

69
Chartres cathedral.
Buttresses
of the chevet,
ca. 1212–20.

nological prowess, its particular configuration, however, dramatizing the message by means of fantastic elation and thrill. But even the routine tall office building common since the close of the nineteenth century offers the opportunity for such sensations.

Offers the opportunity—but only occasionally exploits it. Except for the vertiginous expanse of glass on the outside wall, the typical habitable space in recently built office towers seldom differs much from similar spaces at ground level. Some earlier tall buildings drew more from the idea of height. I am thinking here, not of the progeny of Louis Sullivan's Guaranty Building, but rather of a few towers from the late twenties that combine the massing of Eliel Saarinen's Tribune Tower project with Art Deco detail. Some of these include a profusion of balconies—Seattle's Northern Life Tower of 1929–30 by Albertson, Wilson, and

70

Albertson, Richardson, and Wilson, Northern Life (now Seattle) Tower, Seattle, 1929–30. Projecting, recessed, and sectional-change balconies occur at floors 3, 5, 7, 13, 14, 17, 19, 23, 24, and 25.

Richardson is one of the better examples (figure 70). Balconies in such buildings confer significant advantages. They dramatize the thrill of elevation by offering the occupant exposure to the sky as well as the opportunity to lean over the edge of the architectural precipice for the thrill of a view over the void. Balconies are also free from the refuge conferred by the ceiling plane and the three walls of solid material of interior spaces. Because a balcony opens to extensive space on four of the six sides of the spatial cube, it increases the sense of peril. I suspect that like the prospect-symbolizing terrace adjoining the living space in a house, such balconies are valued even if not used, as places of potential thrill, to be converted to actuality as we choose. Recent interest in complex and variegated forms for tall urban buildings has reintroduced the possibility of such balconies. Although they are year-round habitable spaces only in the most favorable climates, even there they are unsuited to the normal activities possible in an interior space. But they need neither heat nor air conditioning, neither glazing nor finished floors nor walls nor ceiling, and in typical tall building usage they seldom need electrical services. Cantilevered balconies, structurally straightforward in either steel or concrete, are unlikely in lower floors because of projection over the street below—although they are possible, cleverly worked in, for example, at the third floor of the Northern Life Tower. But in many cities there are now incentives for what is sometimes called sculptured massing, which usually encompasses a progressive recessing of the wall plane as the building ascends. Each such recession is an opportunity for balconies or terraces; figure 30 in fact looks toward a terrace generated from just such a condition. It may be that the time for the office balcony has returned.

Interior Peril

Elevated passageways of one sort or another across or adjacent to large interior spaces give another opportunity to exploit peril. Although these are largely independent of site or program preconditions, a building that includes them needs at least a generous interior volume. There are medieval examples in the galleries and the walkable triforia of any Romanesque or Gothic cathedral (figure 71). English builders in the fourteenth and fifteenth centuries seem to have been especially interested in constructing aerial walkways: there is one across a transept at Lincoln (figure 72), and there are thrilling catwalks across the great east window and in the suppressed transept at York Minster (figure 73). London's St. Paul's has a walkway around the interior perimeter of the dome looking out over the void of its crossing, and there are many other similar examples of its era. The advent of modern materials has enormously increased

71
Laon. The gallery
(© Jack O'Connell).

72
Lincoln cathedral,
1180–1311.
The triforium bridge.

73
York Minster, 1230–
1475. The southeast
transept, with
catwalks at center.

74
George H. Wyman,
the Bradbury Building,
Los Angeles, 1893
(© Norman J.
Johnston).

75
A bridge in a
commercial atrium,
Kobe, ca. 1988.

such opportunities; much longer, more dramatic spans have become commonplace, and the open metal handrails common to such examples only delicately intervene between us and the void across which we move. The iron balconies and stairs of George H. Wyman's Bradbury Building in Los Angeles of 1893 (figure 74) or Henri Labrouste's Bibliothèque Nationale in Paris of 1861–69 offer nineteenth-century versions of Laon, Lincoln, and York; the atrium of figure 75 is an example from the 1980s.

Such stairs and internal balconies are now widespread in public and semipublic buildings. They are less common in the private dwelling; an example such as Eric Owen Moss's house in Los Angeles of 1993, for Linda Lawson and Tracy Westen (figures 76, 77), is all the more important.[19]

76
Eric Owen Moss,
Lawson-Westen house,
Los Angeles, 1993.
The living room
with kitchen and
stair beyond
(© Tom Bonner).

77
Lawson-Westen house.
The view through
the stair downward
to the kitchen
(© Tom Bonner).

78
The pyramid of Zoser,
Saqqara, ca. 2750 B.C.
(© Joan Nilsson).

A Special Case: The Setting for the Hero Myth

Peril in the case of the Napes Needle or the Lawson-Westen house results from a natural or artificial configuration that creates the possibility of a serious or fatal fall. The danger can be managed through the exercise of skill and care at the Napes Needle, or by an architectural feature — the stair with handrail — at the Lawson-Westen house. The peril of other settings immediately recognized as perilous arises rather from the palpable absence of characteristics universally understood to support life. We might call such places settings of deficiency or deprivation; they are for good reason the settings of the hero tale.

Joseph Campbell describes the essential tale repeated over millennia and across continents.[20] The hero leaves a situation of relative comfort to face a dangerous adventure, a trial often involving a descent into the earth or the sea or both; after severe struggle the hero emerges triumphant (even if the adventure claims his or her life, as it often does), leaving for mankind some larger wisdom. Why the repetitive story? For our species, whose instincts are now accompanied by languages through which such stories can be created and recounted, the hero myth tells us that if we are brave enough and wise enough, we have some chance of enduring hardship, even agony, to emerge with greater wisdom, even honor. This is sound counsel for eliciting the best efforts of each individual in the communal group in times of difficulty; hence the societal utility of the hero. Most religions add to the basic theme a message of unparalleled attraction to a survival-seeking creature: if one believes in the hero, interprets correctly his or her vaguely described code (usually a tough job in itself), and follows that code, one survives forever. Such stories demand settings that complement the hero's tribulation by making visibly evident some element of challenge: the setting is deficient, one way or another, in support or reassurance.

The Egyptian desert is utterly hostile to life: it has no water, no food sources, no refuge, no "meadow, grove, and stream." The pyramid is built on the deficient landscape (figure 78). It is at one level a cairn, and although recognizing this identity depends on cognitive knowl-

79
Mycenae,
ca. 1250 B.C.

edge — one has to know that it is a tomb — it touches those with that knowledge, reminding them of that universal longing to be remembered, to have one's life marked. But the austerity of its site and structure suggests a vast distance from life and time; the hero-king within must also, by association, be transcendent.

Such an architecture can do more than express and enhance the hero myth; it can create it. The huge and harsh ruins of the Mycenaean citadels suggested to Homer, and still suggest to us, an age of heroes (figure 79). The lone prairie, the parched desert, the limitless mountains of the American West, landscapes devoid of any symbols of comfort or support, have encouraged and in some degree created a family of American hero myths as ubiquitous and seemingly as durable as the Homeric tales. And not the landscape alone: typically the towns are utterly spare. The church, if any, may make some gesture to stylistic elegance; little else of the town's architecture does. The main street where the hero confirms his status is scruffy dirt; the buildings that line it are of raw weathered boards. Such a setting invites us to invent or enlarge the hero, who will transcend the refugeless and comfortless setting to emerge with a rough wisdom and an elemental nobility.

Louis Kahn's library for Phillips Exeter Academy of 1972 is entered through a modest vestibule known only through exploration or initiation. Moving from it, up the library's double stair, we find the central volume (figure 80), around which the study spaces are ranged. These are refuge spaces, places for books, seating, and study carrels; they are low, narrow, and dark by comparison with the central volume. They utilize Wrightian materials: wood, exquisitely detailed to be pleasurable to the touch; carpet; and brick. One of these refuge spaces also includes, Wright-like, a fireplace. Each of these refuge spaces projects a balcony, also Wright-like, toward the prospect space of the central volume. But in that central volume this library, like Kahn's other great buildings, is not Wrightian at all; is like few other buildings of any time or place. The central space stands apart from the refuge spaces,

80
Louis Kahn, Library,
Phillips Exeter
Academy, Exeter, New
Hampshire, 1972. The
central volume (© The
Kahn Collection, The
Architectural Archives
of the University of
Pennsylvania).

and not only spatially. It is all cool harsh concrete;[21] there is no reassurance of anthropomorphically dimensioned detail, no natural materials warm to the touch and gentle to the eye. The large elemental geometric forms — circle and square — delimit and control the study floors and their balconies at the edges. This central space is a landscape of deficiency — like that of Kahn's Salk Institute at La Jolla of 1959–65 (figure 81), whose study cells, intimate and wood-clad, look to a spare and severe courtyard with only a trickle of water to soften the austerity. At Exeter and Salk we share in microcosm the hero's journey from comfort to challenge.

If such confrontations have any real counterpart in Wright's work, it can only be at Fallingwater, and the comparison is revealing. At Fallingwater the core of the building is refuge of the coziest sort; hazard is external to the warm, snug, reassuring spaces of the haven. At

81
Louis Kahn, the Salk
Institute, La Jolla,
Calif., 1959–65.
The courtyard.

Phillips Exeter and Salk the space of heroic implication is the essence of the architectural composition.

Our most recent monument that on the face of it one might expect to belong to the heroic is the 1980–82 Vietnam Memorial on the Mall in Washington, D.C., by Maya Lin. A polished vertical surface of stone etched with the names of the war dead serves as the edge, a kind of retaining wall, for a gentle but extensive depression cut into the earth (figure 82). The wall thus might be understood as holding back the earth's cover, rejecting interment and so conferring immortality on those whose names are recorded on the earth-restraining surface. But this is not, to me at least, the impression most strongly conveyed. Vincent Scully's comments are perceptive and eloquent: "The ground opens for all of us. We are drawn into it, touching the cool face of death with our hand. We commune with the dead. The ages crowd in with us."[22] Yes, we are drawn into the earth, symbol of the heroic ordeal, and on this journey, our image reflected in the polished wall, we accompany those lost dead, or the names of the lost dead (figure 83). But there is no complementary symbol of heroic attainment. Nothing projects in triumph above the original and still insistent plane of the Mall's surface into the zone of the living. In our memories the time of Vietnam was not heroic nor was the war one of large heroic events, and so this memorial, in its absence of triumphal gestures, seems true to the circumstances it commemorates. It touches our deepest innate predilections, the more so because it is poignantly and meaningfully incomplete.

82
Maya Lin,
the Vietnam Memorial,
Washington, D.C.,
1980–82.

The Vietnam
Memorial.

CATEGORIZING AND
DIFFERENTIATING

PROSPECT AND REFUGE, ENTICEMENT AND PERIL are fundamentally characteristics of habitable spaces; as such they belong to landscape and architecture and their surrogates in pictures or words. We now come to some characteristics that occupy a somewhat different position. They have been repeatedly associated, not with spatial experiences alone, but with many other aesthetic experiences; they are also central to all four essential families of survival behavior. These characteristics have been variously termed "likeness tempered with difference" (Gerard Manley Hopkins);[1] "similitude in dissimilitude" (William Wordsworth);[2] "a pattern that contains the unexpected" (John R. Platt);[3] and "on the one side, order, regularity, simplicity and harmony, and, on the other, disorder, irregularity, complexity and discord" (Jay Appleton).[4] For reasons I explain later, I am going to use the terms "order" and "complexity" for the two sides of the matter; and since, like prospect and refuge, these turn out to be a matched pair, it will often be useful to link them as "ordered complexity" or "complex order." In this chapter I want to explore the relationship of these paired characteristics to architecture, suggesting in the process a more detailed theoretical basis and a more extensive working terminology for critical and creative application.

If these characteristics are ubiquitous to the aesthetic experience, is it not likely that they can be applied to just about any piece of architecture that has had its admirers? Yes, probably—but still there may be a few points worth discussing. For example, what place do these characteristics occupy in the evolutionary argument we have been using? Discussing that point may reveal some of the usefulness these characteristics have held for us, and may thereby clarify what we are predisposed to value in them. Then there is the question of degree: given the value of order and complexity, is more or less of one or the other better or worse? What is the optimal amount? What empirical evidence points to it? Then too there may be different elements to which such characteristics may apply and differences in scale, from a small residential room to an urban space that includes several major buildings. And there may turn out to be distinguishably different ways of experiencing these characteristics, some more pregnant with architectural possibilities than others—and some that present a problem or two.

The Pleasures of Categorizing and Differentiating

Creatures are beset by information. They—most clearly and complicatedly those we call the "higher" animals—must in some way process this information if they are to respond with appropriate behavior. Such processing demands an ability to sort the information into some kind of order, and also to grasp fine distinctions within it.[5]

One most basic sorting task for any creature involves distinguishing its fellow creatures from others; if it cannot manage this, it has little chance of either finding a mate to produce offspring or caring for that mate and offspring. The creature Homo sapiens must be interested in identifying fellow Homo sapiens, and we are. From the earliest times of which there is record we have created and surrounded ourselves with simulations of ourselves. The Venus of Willendorf, perhaps roughly contemporaneous with the advent of language, is one piece of evidence. So are the west portal figures of Chartres cathedral, of later date, that usher us into the place that purports to offer eternal survival (figure 84) and the figure on the southwest corner of the cathedral of Orvieto that, like those at Chartres, is about life-size (figure 85).

These examples of course are literally anthropomorphic. We also see ourselves where we are not; much architectural detail consists of elements suggesting human characteristics in less literal ways. Figure 86 includes several representations of the human figure, and also some bits that suggest parts of the human body but in fact are purely architectural. The classical column, as here, has been interpreted anthropomorphically since Vitruvius,[6] the argument being that its bulging taper and flaring top, in their expression of support, resemble a human figure bearing a burden.[7] Parts of the column, moreover, and many other details of the scene, are similar in size and shape to elements of our bodies. Here one value of the classical tradition may be quite simply stated: it encourages us to order scenes like this according to elements that suggest the component parts of ourselves. But such clues are not the exclu-

84
Chartres. Ushers
(© Douglas and
Jennifer Varey).

85
Orvieto. Three men.

sive property of the classical vocabulary: the pier base in the typical Gothic cathedral (figure 87), for example, is wrapped with moldings at about waist and shoulder height that correlate with the human waists and shoulders that wander by.

But a creature engaging in categorizing behavior must do more than identify its own kind. It must also sort appropriate food sources: herbivores must recognize nourishing vegetable material, predators must have a programmed eye — or nose, or ear — for digestible prey. For most species, threat recognition is also vital. This too depends on properly categorizing information: the zebra may be eaten by the lion eventually, but its odds of getting to offspring-producing age improve if it has a mechanism that sorts lions from wildebeests.

Gerd Sommerhoff believes that such a sorting mechanism is inherent in the human brain.[8] He uses concepts drawn from information theory that posit a relationship between information available and accurate interpretation: increasing the information decreases the

86

The parish church
of Saint John the
Baptist, Burford,
Gloucestershire,

1120 –. Anthropo-
morphic details
(© Dennis Noson).

87

Reims cathedral,
1210 – 90. The south
aisle looking toward
the west front.

number of alternative interpretations. Abundant information from the environment reduces our uncertainty and helps us to predict accurately the conditions of our immediate future. Redundancy — repetition of information — still further improves the chances of accurate interpretation. Thus the obvious survival value of an interest in adequate and redundant information; a brain structure that "likes" those characteristics should be selected for.

We seem to have such a brain; we seem to like informational abundance and redundancy. But what are the processes by which this liking happens? Sommerhoff believes our brain analyzes information from the senses in terms of "what-leads-to-what expectancies"; he calls this concept "the Conditional Expectancy Hypothesis."[9] The brain expects future event-and-image sets to be like event-and-image sets previously experienced. When repetition of previous experience seems likely, the brain readies itself to reexperience the set. If expectancies are confirmed, the model is reinforced, with a resultant sensation of pleasure. (If expectations are violated, the brain adjusts its model and presumably thereafter expects, and is pleased by, the modified version.) Sommerhoff calls this "cognitive consonance."

> Consider a simple figure or shape with a high degree of order, like a circle or a regularly shaped fern or flower. Such regular figures or shapes have a high redundancy because as the eye runs from one part of the circle or flower to the next it meets no surprises: what it sees looking at one part has to some extent already been suggested by what it saw looking at a previous part.[10]

By such means, then, and with considerable accuracy, we place the subjects of our sensory perceptions in ordered categories. By such means we also find pleasure in subjects — flowers, for example — that intrinsically possess a "high degree of order." But what is a "high degree of order"? How is it order? What does "order" mean in such circumstances?

Establishing groupings of similar objects — wildebeests, or many flowers — requires sensitivity to the repetition of like characteristics in similar arrangements, as Sommerhoff suggests. This repetition apparently need not present identical or even markedly similar patterns on the retina, since objects change in retinal image as they take different positions relative to the viewer. The mind, perhaps working in part from experience, perhaps in part as a consequence of biologically prepared learning, must do considerable interpretation to correlate a present front view of an animal with a prior side or quarter view, and to place that animal in the right category. Nor, apparently, need images on the retina be of repetitive size; large variations are inevitable because both viewing distance and size can vary from one example of a group to another. Nevertheless a flower seen from a novel distance and a novel angle is interpreted as belonging to a category created in the viewer's mind — not necessarily a human viewer's mind — through encounters with other flowers; the immediate flower consists of parts like those already known as characterizing that category of information. In such an instance a sense of order derives from classifying information as a function of repetition of features despite differing retinal patterns.

88

Nature's fractal games: Italian broccoli. The overall conical shape is repeated in the smaller cones that proceed in helical arrangement around the large one. These in turn are helically wrapped by littler cones, which in turn are wrapped by . . . and so on to the least size the eye can make out and, presumably, beyond.

This process can work hierarchically. Individual petals of a daisy are not just similar to those of another daisy; they are also like one another. And they relate to one another by being spaced at regular intervals. So the complete daisy repeats not only other complete daisies but also, within itself, its own constituent elements and the interval relationship between them. Again one can imagine "conditional expectancy" at work: the mind perceives the daisy as like other daisies and is satisfied; notes in the daisy the petal, then two or three the same with a like interval between them; anticipates a continuation of this additional hierarchically nested organization; and experiences satisfaction in this realization. Is this one reason for the value we attach to flowers? Fractal geometries are an elegant epitome of this hierarchical characteristic.[11] Italian broccoli, one of the most wonderful of natural fractal geometries, can produce in Homo sapiens that most honest evidence of pleasure, a smile or a laugh (figure 88). Its infinite progression of hierarchical order generates delight.

A further point can be made about the appeal of repetitive intervals. In ourselves and the world around us many events occur in intervals as regular as the daisy's petals: our walking or running steps are rhythmic, as are those of the animal world; even birds that arrest wing movement to glide on the wind resume wing movement to a regular rhythm. Our heartbeat and breathing are rhythmic, and so are the crashing of the ocean surf, the chirping of crickets, the cries of many birds — even the sounds of creatures of the sea. Through such complementary associations, repetition of interval may enrich the satisfaction of an isolated feature, a total image, or an event.

Most creatures, however, are selected for the ability to make some fine distinctions. Predators, including ourselves, are more successful if in considering similar individuals in a category of prey — woolly mammoths, for example — they are attuned to differences in size (the smaller, the weaker) and in agility (the slower, the more easily caught). Fellow members of one's own species have to be recognized as more or less like one another, but many species must also recognize mother, brother, male, female, friend, enemy, adult, and offspring.

> When the goslings hatch, and especially just before they're ready to leave the nest, the mother is delicately attuned to the nuances of their sounds, looks and (perhaps) smells. She has learned about her chicks. Now, she knows her own very well, and would not confuse them with someone else's goslings, however similar they may seem to a human observer. In species of birds where mix-ups are likely, where the young may fledge and mistakenly land in a neighboring nest, the machinery for maternal recognition and discrimination is even more elaborate.[12]

Chickens work out a pecking order to establish hierarchy within the group, valuable because it makes further time-consuming and destructive fighting unnecessary. This means that stupid though chickens may seem to us, they not only distinguish themselves from other creatures—foxes, for example—but also routinely distinguish chicken A from chicken B from chicken C.[13] Attention to fine distinctions in inanimate material also brings rewards. In a group of environments capable of sustaining life—trees, for example, for most birds—it helps to distinguish those that sustain remarkably well from those whose sustaining potential is meager. Many creatures also distinguish their personal habitat from that typical of their species: birds returning to their individual nests offer an everyday example; the return of salmon to spawn in the exact river of their conception or of ocean-dwelling turtles to the island of their birth presents a more dramatic one.

So the ordering behavior of creatures is commonly and necessarily accompanied by attention to fine degrees of difference or variety.

> Comparative psychologists have found that, in almost every species studied, animals will work to be exposed to novel sensory stimuli. Indeed, "stimulus novelty" is the most universal reinforcer of behaviour which is known. . . . Recent experiments strongly suggest that when monkeys work to look at pictures they do so because the picture presents them with a challenge to incorporate new material into their model of the world: pictures of familiar objects hold their attention far less long than pictures of objects for which they have no readily available category. But while they do not spend long on thoroughly familiar things, neither, I should say, are they interested in looking at a total jumble. . . . human babies who have been made familiar with a particular "abstract" visual pattern take pleasure in seeing new patterns which are minor transformations of the original. . . . [but are not] attracted to stimuli which are wholly unrelated to what they have already seen.[14]

If we return to the premise that survival-advantageous conditions and conditions Homo sapiens likes ought to match, we should not be surprised to find that ordering (not "looking at a total jumble") and distinguishing (seeking "a challenge to incorporate new material into [our] model of the world") are characteristics of our creative and appreciative activities. If we turn from observer to observed, we see that pleasurable phenomena or artifacts are likely to show corresponding characteristics of *order* and *complexity*.[15]

Having got this far, we can see that there is an even more general and ubiquitous circumstance in which liking complexity, and liking to find ordered categories in it, would have been advantageous to our ancestors. A complex natural surrounding is probably rich in quantity and variety of resources; a simple surrounding is probably deficient. Creatures with a predilection for complex environments who make sense of them efficiently maximize their resource options and so have greater odds of reproductive success than those with neither a preference for the complex environment nor the skill to process its information. In this way a predilection for complex environments, and for sorting out the information they present, will be whetted over generations.

Complexity and order, under various near-synonyms, have long been thought central to the aesthetic experience; this centrality may well explain what has been called the "will to form," *Kunstwollen*; "there is something in man which leads him to find pleasure in formal beauty."[16] If we accept that natural selection, in a sense, "designs" species, we may acknowledge that we have been designed to like order and complexity. The value we assign to them in the events and images of our lives is therefore neither occasional, exceptional, nor trivial; it is pervasive and fundamental.

I would take a moment to defend the terms "order" and "complexity." In the first paragraph of this chapter I cited others that have been used: "likeness tempered with difference," "similitude in dissimilitude," "a pattern that contains the unexpected," and "on the one side, order, regularity, simplicity and harmony, and, on the other, disorder, irregularity, complexity and discord." In relation to many families of aesthetic experience—music or poetry or architecture—several of these phrases seem inaccurate. I do not see that music, for example, needs "dissimilitude," while "difference" seems severely inadequate. Nor does "disorder" or "irregularity" quite fill the bill; those terms seem off the mark for many examples in the arts. I realize that the term "complexity" can also be flawed because some aesthetic experiences seem to include simplicity, in one or another interpretation of that word; but I would argue, at least provisionally, that what seems to be simplicity may more usefully be called order; and that on careful reflection such examples will be seen to include complexity as well.

As I have implied, the two terms are not opposites. The opposite of order is disorder; of complexity, simplicity. By contrast, order and complexity are allies, necessarily allies, in fact, and can be semantically joined as *ordered complexity* or *complex order*. Sometimes joining them in this way is convenient; at other times it is more useful to consider them separately. But they can never be assumed opposites.

Nicholas Humphrey mentions their role in stimulating a sense of formal beauty in a field where one might not expect it: "At an extreme among scholars, pure mathematicians find their own kind of beauty in the relations among abstract numerical ideas."[17] In an extraordinary essay the mathematician Henri Poincaré has stated his own case: he assigns characteristics of order and complexity to mathematical creativity, considers the unconscious its source, and asserts that the process yields beauty. He concludes:

> It may be surprising to see emotional sensibility invoked *a propos* of mathematical demonstrations which, it would seem, can interest only the intellect. This would be to forget the feeling of mathematical beauty, of the harmony of numbers and forms, of geometric elegance. This is a true esthetic feeling that all real mathematicians know, and surely it belongs to emotional sensibility.
>
> Now, what are the mathematical entities to which we attribute this character of beauty and elegance, and which are capable of developing in us a sort of esthetic emotion? They are those whose elements are harmoniously disposed so that the mind without effort can embrace their totality while realizing the details.[18]

Poetry is an order of rhythm, sounds, or both. Even at the elemental level of nursery rhymes — "Mary had a little lamb" — rhythm is evident; it is one reason for their universal appeal. A subtler order lies in the sounds. I take a line from Coleridge's "Kubla Khan": "Through caverns measureless to man." The fulcrum is the *u* of measureless; equidistant to either side in almost architectural symmetry are the hard *s* sounds of caverns and -less; the soft *a*'s of caverns and man; and the soft *e*'s of caverns and -less. The *m*'s of measureless and man are not quite symmetrical, while at a greater remove there are the *n*'s of caverns and man. Usually rhythm is abstracted easily from other characteristics of a poem; the order of sounds is more difficult to isolate because closely bound up with cognitive content. Yet subconsciously we perceive both, and the sounds, at least, we perceive as an order of some complexity. This is characteristic of many phrases that remain in memory. Lincoln's "of the people, by the people, and for the people, shall not perish" is musically rhythmic in the stresses that naturally arise from its syllables, while the sequence of seven *p*'s establishes a secondary coherence of consonant sounds. Churchill's "Never in the field of human conflict was so much owed by so many to so few" arrests the ear and the mind through the rhythmic recurrence of the hard *s*'s and long *o*'s, complemented by the soft *i* of conflict, the *u* of much, the *a* and *y* of many, and the flowing *ew* that closes the phrase.[19]

To this I add my own experience of hearing poetry whose appeal depended entirely on sounds and rhythms because the language, and therefore its cognitive meaning, were unknown to me. Examples include Clytemnestra's speech on the message from Troy in Aeschylus's *Agamemnon*, in classical Greek; Dies Irae, in Latin; and the prologue to *Beowulf* in Old English. They seem almost music — certainly the temptation in reading or speaking them is to give them a musical character. Robert Fitzgerald says of the *Aeneid*, "As a poem it is carried onward victoriously by its own music."[20]

Which brings us to music. Music almost universally includes a complex order of rhythm: an assemblage of rhythmic beats, stresses that organize the beats into meters, and usually additional rhythmic material that builds further complexities into a rhythmic structure. In much — most — music there are complex orders of tones as well: sequences of tones including multiple simultaneous tones relate to one another through differing but complementary resonances. To these complex structures of sound can be added the complementary resonances of each tone taken individually, and the distinctions of instrumental and vocal timbre. Then there is the development and re-development, repetition and contrast, of thematic material. Overlaid on this already fantastically complex order are the structured changes in pace and volume, "the fortes and pianissimos, the crescendos, decrescendos, tempos, accelerandos, ritardandos, fermatas, that transform mere rhythmic, melodic, and harmonic patterns into something with the power to move us."[21] Music, then, is complexly ordered sound. The definition seems inappropriately austere for such a rich human creation; still, under that definition music has been a part of all cultures the earth has ever seen. Tastes differ; your complexly ordered sound may not be mine; but all Homo sapiens seem determined to experience complexly ordered sound in one form or another. Dance too can be sparely defined as complexly ordered human movement, and that too all Homo sapiens like and have liked.

Because of their generality and ubiquity these characteristics alone help in analyzing

89
Himeji castle,
near Kyoto,
ca. 1600. A wall.

many settings. A complex assemblage of natural material frames the view of a wall at Himeji
Castle (figure 89). The eye moves compulsively to the wall, which holds attention because of
its easily grasped order of elements and intervals. The eye then searches the wall for more information—and finds abundant complexities in each constituent element.

It might be soundly argued that this view would be less intriguing if we removed the fabricated element, the wall. The scene is one of many examples—including most of those cited
in this book—in which a fabricated element in the composition increases the appeal of the
image. Why should this be so? Although this wall at Himeji could serve as a vehicle for an
answer to the question, the Alhambra, as shown in figure 15, serves even better, including as
it does a much greater proportion of architectural material. The Alhambra as shown in that
illustration shares archetypal characteristics with its natural counterparts the grove and
meadow in ways described in Chapter 2. But—to bring it into this chapter's discussion—it
presents those characteristics by means of a complex order more obvious, but not less rich,
than that of nature. The order of the architectural material at the Alhambra—column elements, intervals, ornamental units, roof slopes, tiles—is more easily discerned and more exactly repetitive than its natural equivalents in the images it presents to the retina, while the
complexities equal those of nature in drawing the eye into infinite processes of discovery. One
could maintain—with some supporting evidence— that such an architectural image in its
combination of complexity and order, prospect and refuge, may sometimes equal or exceed
the innate appeal of similar combinations in nature.[22] There can be little doubt that we originally created and still create our other art forms—music being the clearest example—to
fulfill our lust for complex order. It is possible, even probable, that this purpose underlies the
creation of architecture too.

Order and complexity are not just comfortable allies; they are necessary allies. Order without complexity is monotony, and is felt to be that in the deadly repetition of much speculative American housing of the late 1940s (figure 90). Color would help this desperate scene and, for reasons that belong in the preceding chapter, plantings would too. Nevertheless the image as seen here tells us something: we need just such enriching conditions and grope for whatever enrichment we can draw from the few curves of the street layout. Ordinary people voting with their mortgages have made roughly the same point, with the consequence that in ensuing years and to the present such developments have increasingly offered varying facade treatments, choices of floor plan, occasionally some options in finish materials. Apparently the market demands and rewards the provision of some complexity as relief from too-simple order. Professional response has often attacked the banality of such "complexities" in these projects, and with some justice. Horizons richer than such approaches even begin to suggest may help to explain the renewed popularity of older neighborhoods and perhaps the movement to preserve them for their accretions and variety, which give the mind more to discover. Either case, however, supports our need for more than order alone—as do conversations among occupants of similar dwelling units in residential developments and condominiums, which typically focus and expand on the obvious likenesses, and the often quite minute differences, among similar units.[23]

Complexity without order, however, is no more satisfying than order without complexity: "Scenes that [are] difficult to organize and interpret were not only rated low in preference;

they were actually resented." [24] The ubiquitous American commercial strip is an example. Its best-known defense, *Learning from Las Vegas*, [25] purports to describe an order within the seeming chaos. Whether in the actual setting the order is convincing to the eye remains for me an open question, but clearly even in that instance order is seen as requisite to the argument. There too the market has forced the issue: commercial strips, and much more often malls, are increasingly subject to rules for architectural consistency.

Complex Order and the Single Building

Consider the nave of Exeter cathedral (figure 91). The eye is continually reminded of order by the repetitive bays and, less obviously, by the kinship of elements in each bay. In the lowest story — the nave arcade — the eye sees the pier shaft clusters and arch moldings as interrelated; the intermediate story — the triforium — repeats a permutation of the nave arcade at smaller size; above it the vaulting ribs are cousins to the shafts and moldings below; and the uppermost windows — the clerestory — are brothers to the nave arcade with which we started. All share a texture and scale. We grasp and are reassured by a cohering sameness of things. Yet the vault rib cluster is *not* like the pier: its linear elements diverge as they ascend, and so necessarily frame masonry panels of continuously varying breadth. The intersections of the ribs are marked by ornamental bosses; no two are alike. The eye drifts back down to the nave pier, to the springing point of the arcade. Just above each pier capital is an ornamented tall projection, the corbel; each of these is unique, yet each is surmounted by a shaft cluster, identical from bay to bay, that repeats at smaller size the cluster of shafts of the pier below. The nave arcade arches are made up of two intersecting circular arcs; those of the triforium are made up of four arcs, with pairs intersecting to create a cusp. The clerestory windows are framed within two arcs that echo the nave arcade, but within these the stonework, the tracery, that holds the glass is worked out in a profusion of arcs that yield both pointed and cusped arches, and much else too. (The complex order of the Gothic cathedral may itself reflect two other preoccupations of medieval society. A fundamental objective of medieval scholasticism, culminating in Aquinas's *Summa,* was to elucidate the unified ordering of God's universe in a scheme sufficiently broad, supple, and inclusive to reconcile the infinite diversities of that universe. And a fundamental objective of musical composition in the period was the increasingly complex ordering of sound that eventually became Western polyphonic music.) [26]

103

91
Exeter cathedral.
The nave looking east,
Devon, 1270–1470.

Exeter illustrates these characteristics unusually well, but a similar discussion could be built around any of the buildings of which it is such a good representative: Beverley Minster (figure 92), or Reims (figure 87), or Orvieto (figure 3), or innumerable contemporaneous smaller parish churches across Europe. One could also cite examples from quite different historical periods: the lateral facades of Michelangelo's Campidoglio of the 1560s (figure 93) or the interior of the Zimmerman brothers' Wieskirche in Bavaria of the 1750s or Antonio Gaudi's Casa Batlló in Barcelona of 1905—all would illustrate the point.

Or would illustrate it in the solid material of architecture. Architectural space, however, can be complexly ordered too. Consider an example already discussed in another context: Wright's Cheney house of 1904 (figure 94; see also figure 20). Its living room is bounded by— created by—the fireplace recess on the one side and the range of French doors to the terrace opposite, and by piers and some built-in bookcases on either flank. North of this living space is the dining space, created by two exterior walls, one interior one, and the piers and book-

cases. South is the music space, created by the same features mirror-imaged. Three spaces are delineated by substantial and clear architectural features. But when the eye looks upward, it finds a ceiling whose sloped planes echo those of the roof, as seen in figure 19. This ceiling (indicated by paired dashed lines in the plan, figure 94) includes, without interruption, the entire breadth of the house, uniting dining and music spaces with the central part of the living space (see figure 21). So the spatial composition of this house can be understood in two quite different ways: as a large central living space that includes fireplace and French doors, with smaller music and dining spaces on its flanks; or as a single laterally extended volume off which, at its midpoint, are a recess for a fireplace and a recess for French doors. Such complexly ordered spaces of later date can be seen in Botta's house at Stabio (figures 22–25), in the condominium by Gordon Walker (figures 29–31), in the Lawson-Westen house by Eric Owen Moss (figures 76, 77), and in many other examples. Even so, Wright's Cheney house is remarkable for the evident order within which its spatial complexities are structured.

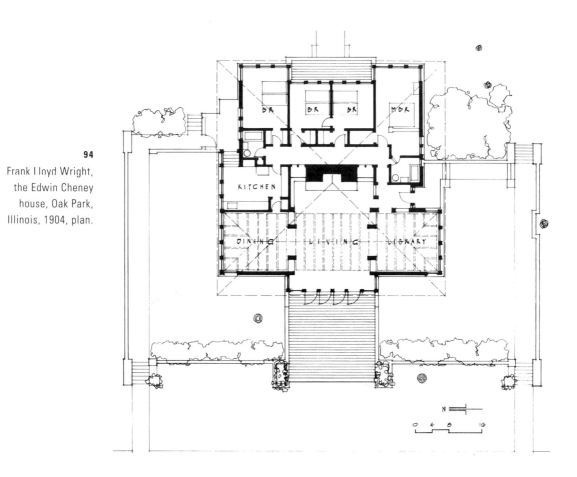

94
Frank Lloyd Wright,
the Edwin Cheney
house, Oak Park,
Illinois, 1904, plan.

One could also argue that the bait in the enticement experience is complexly ordered material partly hidden from view. The vista from the narrow city street toward the facade of Orvieto cathedral (figure 38), for example, tells us that interesting discoveries await by presenting to the eye abundant and unmistakable evidence that a body of very complexly ordered architectural material lies just ahead. The appeal of such a promise in a city street leads us to the matter of the townscape.

Complex Order and the Townscape

Although the Piazza San Marco, a frequent tourist destination, together with its *piazzetta*, is one of the more expensive places in the world to visit, people willingly spend money to place themselves in it for a few hours or a few days. It is also a remarkably good example of a complex order that pervades several seemingly dissimilar buildings done by a number of different architects over a considerable stretch of time.[27] The compositional theme was set by the two earliest extant buildings, whose facades together make up the eastern wall of piazza and *piazzetta*.

St. Mark's, the Ducal Chapel, is of indeterminate date but primarily eleventh century (figure 95). What are the compositional characteristics of its facade? One can think of it as three layers, or strata. The lowest consists of five dark arches deeply cut into the facade. Each of the five arches, however, is really a nested pair, since a less obvious smaller arch, delineated by its own enframement, is contained within each larger one. Above these is a planar story with no deep relief and no particular modeling of surface except for the insignificant tiny

95
The Ducal Chapel (St. Mark's), Venice, 985–. The Piazza facade.

96
The Ducal Palace,
Venice, 1309–1424.
The facade toward the
piazzetta; the Ducal
Chapel beyond.

openings. Above that is an orgy of pinnacles, porches, arcades, and statues. The fourteenth-century Ducal Palace (figure 96) immediately to the south has a base similar to that of the chapel—a deeply shadowed arcade made up of arches of two sizes; but these arches, unlike those of the chapel, are in two stories, stacked not nested, in a precise width relationship of 1:2. Above is an expanse of planar surface punctuated by windows. Since these have to provide working interior light for the palace, they are necessarily larger than the small openings in the planar portion of the chapel, but they have unusually modest frames that hardly interrupt the planarity of this zone. At the center, as at the chapel, is a more emphatic feature, an ornamented panel. Along the roofline is the elaborate crown of the strange fish-spine cornice. The characteristics shared by these two earliest buildings—a deeply shadowed arcade, large and small arches, a much simpler planar surface above, and an elaborate skyline—state the theme observed in various permutations by all the ensuing buildings.

The Procuratie Vecchie of about 1465 accounts for most of the north side of the piazza (figure 97). Because it is usually considered one of the weaker buildings of the group, it is of special interest here, for it perpetuates and plays variations on a theme that seems to have been understood even by one of the less talented Venetian architects. The ground story is a deeply shadowed arcade. In the story above, the arcade bay is halved, emulating the stacked 1:2 relationship of the palace and the nested equivalent of the chapel. The next story is identical; the building program must have demanded a third story with significant daylighting, so the designer cloned the second story—an uninspired but serviceable decision. Above, a heavy, richly modeled attic story and cornice relate that zone to the upper portions of the two prior buildings, with reasonable success.

For the Library of St. Mark, Jacopo Sansovino, in 1536, again treated the ground story as a deeply shadowed arcade, overlaid by a colonnade of attached half-columns carrying a Doric entablature — the ornamented horizontal band just under the balustrade (figure 98). In the story above, attached half-round columns repeat the colonnade of the first floor; this repetition may be Sansovino's nod of respect to the two identical stories of the Procuratie Vecchie. But behind this repeated theme Sansovino realized a brilliant idea: he introduced what is, in effect, a second facade whose column spacing — and therefore arch radius — are half those of the first-story facade (figure 99). In this way he has repeated the two-floors-the-same theme of the Procuratie Vecchie, and at the same time has revisited the Ducal Palace's stacked arcades in a 1:2 relationship. Above, a richly modeled attic and the statues above the balustrade evoke the fish-spine cornice opposite.

Sansovino also did the Logetta on the east face of the Campanile (figure 100). He had just one floor to work with; no chance here for rhythmic permutations in superimposed bays.

97
The Procuratie
Vecchie, Venice,
ca. 1465.

98
Jacopo Sansovino, the
Library of St. Mark,
Venice, 1536.

99
The Library.
Three bays.

100
Jacopo Sansovino,
the Logetta, 1537–
45 (Patrick Young

© 1991 University
of Michigan Slide
Distribution).

He put the two bay widths, in the now-canonical 1:2 relationship, side by side, and above these designed the heaviest imaginable attic story. The vista from the juncture of piazza and *piazzetta*, with the library beyond, offers a convincing example of complex order within each design but also in the relationship between them (figure 101). In spite of this success Sansovino changed the motif for the south facade. Instead of the attic story, he built an odd arch with a blind oculus at center, and even stranger half-oculi at the spring points (figure 100), all of this above a repetition of the window motif he had invented for the second floor of the library. Why the change? Seen from the lagoon this seaward facade of the Logetta is companion to the seaward facade of the Ducal Chapel, whose strange blind oculi and arches of varied widths it echoes (figure 102).

Early in this chapter I quoted Nicholas Humphrey's observation that young Homo sapiens, familiar with a certain visual pattern, "take pleasure in seeing new patterns which are

101
The Library and the
Logetta. Variations
on a theme.

102
The Ducal Chapel.
A portion of the south
(seaward) facade.

103
Arlington Row, Bibury,
Gloucestershire,
seventeenth century (?).
Complex order in a
footpathscape
(© Dennis Noson).

minor transformations of the original. . . . [but are not] attracted to stimuli which are wholly unrelated to what they have already seen." The Piazza San Marco is a sophisticated instance of several such transformations, each new image presenting novel elements and relationships that also develop from and relate to what we have already seen. In this sense such settings have a commonality with poetry and music that goes beyond aphorism and romanticism. A similar approach can be applied to vernacular environments. Peter Smith has pointed out that the cityscape of Amsterdam is ordered by repetitive rhythms of chimneys, gables and roof slopes, and ranks of similarly proportioned windows at similar intervals, to which one might add the repeated use of a narrow range of building materials.[28] Any street in an Italian hilltown or Cotswold village could illustrate similar repetitive characteristics. Arlington Row in Bibury, Gloucestershire (figure 103), presents to the eye seemingly repeated elements and seemingly repeated intervals — doors, windows, dormers, gables, chimneys — whose multitudinous minor variations make each iteration as different from any other, and as alike, as individuals of the same species.

104
Machu Picchu
(© Norman J.
Johnston).

Complex Order and the Site

Machu Picchu (figure 104) exemplifies such an interaction between nature and architectural construct. It is a specialized case because it depends on an unusually rich topography: the verdant sculptural shapes of the mountain saddle on which the city was built provide a dramatic complexity against which the repetitive terraces establish an order of elemental clarity. The magical appeal of the whole depends, in part at least, on the complexities that result when these insistently ordered strata are adapted to the voluptuous site.

In the chaos of present-day Athens (figure 105) the eye settles with relief on the eroded order of the Acropolis. The first impression (figure 106) is of like coloration; the structures rise on the rock as a monochromatic sculptural presence. (This was less true in antiquity when many temple details were painted, but even then much of the Pentelic marble of the buildings was exposed, certainly enough to tie their coloration to that of the rock, as now.) Simultaneously the buildings are seen to consist of many verticals and horizontals—verticals with

105
Athens. A view from
an ordinary street
toward the Acropolis.

113

tops of more detailed shape, horizontals with striated detailed ornamentation—with the occasional sloping line. But art historians have repeatedly pointed out that the order is complemented by complexity, and the eye immediately perceives this too. The irregular forms of the rock are juxtaposed with the structural regularity of buildings that themselves have become irregular over time. The constituent elements of the buildings vary in size, and the eye soon registers the differing details and differing proportions of these differently sized elements. The dominant building, the Parthenon, is unique in its intrinsic complexity (figure 107). It alone among Greek Doric temples includes all the "refinements" of the art history books. The facades incline slightly inward on all sides; the base (styobate) and the entablature (the horizontal band above the columns) arch upward very slightly. The diameters of the corner columns are slightly greater than those of their neighbors. All columns are carved with an extraordinarily gentle bulge (entasis) in the subtle taper of the shaft; and the corner columns, and those immediately next to them as well, are slightly more closely spaced than the intervening columns along sides and end facades, a rare characteristic called double contraction. Many of these subtle variations in both element and interval occur in other temples; the presence of the whole array is unique to the Parthenon. Some have maintained that these "refinements" are there to counter optical illusions, yet the eye sees them readily enough, and perhaps intuitively sees them for what they are, enlivening complexities within an ordered totality.[29] The individual characteristics of the buildings, and the relation-

114

107
The Parthenon,
Athens, 447–432 B.C.
The west facade.

ship between buildings and site that the Acropolis illustrates so well can be found in degree elsewhere, at Delphi, for example, or Vassis, or other less sculptural sites such as Olympia. But even among such distinguished compatriots the Athenian grouping is a remarkably good example of natural and architectural complex order working in concert.

The partly ruined state of this building group may also contribute to its appeal. Each building on the Acropolis retains considerable evidence of its original ordered configuration, but enough has been subtracted by time and mishap to necessitate an act of mental completion of the form. That we seem to find interest and satisfaction in this exercise makes survival sense, for in the natural setting of long ago we must have been impelled, to our advantage, to discern and complete partly revealed configurations of predator or prey, danger or supportive resource: if we saw through the foliage evidences of a configuration that, completed in the mind, we could identify as a tiger, we would have obtained some helpful information. And so by extension, perhaps, the appeal of ruins. But in any case enough must be apparent to the eye to make possible a reasonably accurate completion of the figure. Sites that present only foundation patterns in the grass may be of archaeological value, but they lack clues that can draw the eye and mind into the image-completing game. The immediate sensory rewards belong to sites such as Fountains Abbey or the Basilica of Constantine — or the Athenian Acropolis — where visual evidence adequately supports the pleasurable exercise.[30]

Complex Order as a Function of Movement

The Acropolis or the Piazza San Marco can be understood, by and large, from a single position. One must turn around, of course, or move a few steps, wander a bit, but one stays more or less within the same viewing space, from which all permutations can be seen. There are other cases in which apprehension of complex order requires a significant change of spatial position; not everything can be seen from one viewpoint. One must move through a sequence of spaces, and such movement necessarily takes place over time. Filippo Brunelleschi's Pazzi Chapel in Florence of 1439 is one of the better-known and more important buildings of the early Renaissance. To understand its complex order, one must move from one defined space to another. But as one moves, the original postulation of the order is lost to view and must be held in the memory as the viewer moves through a sequence of variations on the theme.

The chapel's porch facade consists of six Corinthian columns framing five bays (figure 108). The pairs of bays to each side of the center are surmounted by an entablature, the hor-

108
Filippo Brunelleschi,
the Pazzi Chapel,
Florence, 1439–.
The porch facade.

109
The Pazzi Chapel.
The inner wall of
the porch facade
(© Cory Crocker).

izontal band whose middle stratum is ornamented by a series of roundels. The central bay is somewhat wider and is arched, the arch springing from the top of the entablature. (Above, a second story masks transverse vaults beyond at right and left: paired pilasters acknowledge the theme below. The central two pairs, however, force the arch to rest, visually, on two points. Brunelleschi, pioneer that he was, often faced problems that had no ready answers. Occasionally he found less-than-ideal solutions.) The theme, then, is five bays, the lateral pairs with entablature, the central bay wider and arched. In four permutations it informs all the architectural material that lies beyond, but only one of the permutations can be seen from the porch, and the porch facade will be hidden from view when the remaining permutations are encountered.

The first permutation is the inner porch wall, seen in figure 108. Its composition is obviously based on the columnar facade, but walls with windows occur where the voids of the side bays were; pilasters replace columns; and while the central bay remains wide, the entablature of the flanking bays continues across it. We enter the chapel through the doors in the central bay and find that the inside of this entry wall is the second permutation. The inner side is much like the outer, including pilasters and the entablature across the central bay (figure 109), but in this central bay the arch of the porch facade, no longer in view, reappears in its original dimensions, with tympanum between entablature and arch. A new feature—a concentric but much larger arch—springs from the intermediate pilasters of each of the

flanking bays. When we turn around, we find on the opposite wall the third permutation (figure 110). The wall just described is repeated, including the larger central arch, but panels replace windows in lateral bays, and the middle bay is again an open arch — no entablature — as in the original porch facade. Each of the four planes perpendicular to the path of movement — columnar facade, porch wall, interior entry wall, and apse wall — is a unique version of the original theme encountered on approach, and only two such versions at most are visible from any given point along the path of movement. Yet in one version or another the compositional theme is available to the eye at every point.

The side walls of the interior represent the fourth and most radical permutation. They repeat only the central three bays, minus the doors, of the entry wall (figure 111). They are equally close cousins to the middle three bays of the apse wall, with wall and entablature replacing the central void. These side walls thus culminate in an arch whose span is that of the middle three bays of the transverse walls. Within this large arch is the smaller one, which, through simple processes of geometry, is identical to the central arch of the originating porch facade.

Furthermore, as we move through and among these planes, we move under a sequence of three domes. The diameter of the first, above the center of the porch, and of the last, above

111
The Pazzi Chapel.
The lateral wall.

the altar, is established by the width of the central transverse bay. The diameter of the one above the major interior space is established by the combined widths of the central three bays of the transverse walls, which are, of course, exactly replicated by the end walls. So these domes constitute another series of permutations on the originating theme, while movement along the obvious axial path proceeds from a space with a dome of diameter A to one with a dome of diameter B to one with a dome of diameter A (figure 112); so the building holds a hidden symmetry that again can be grasped only through movement.

It has long been believed that Greek and Roman architects consciously developed a relation between the dimensions of various parts of a building that was based on a multiple of the column diameter. If this is so, Brunelleschi carried the idea much further, relating not only individual architectural elements but also groups of elements that are revealed over time by movement through the spatial sequence. This dynamic revelation of relationships is especially interesting since Brunelleschi is often considered the most static of architectural composers. His follower Leon Battista Alberti says nothing about this characteristic in his extensive writings — nothing about movement that reveals order or ordered images held in the mind — and to be fair, we would not expect him to. But at least one of Alberti's buildings, the Church of Sant'Andrea in Mantua, begun in 1470, works in much the same way. Alberti

based the motif for the interior lateral walls on the facade, which, like that of the Pazzi Chapel, is lost to view when one moves to the interior, so again the relationship between interior and exterior depends on associations in memory.

Brunelleschi's late Church of Santo Spirito illustrates a different issue, the apprehension, over time and through movement, of complexity rather than order. At his earlier Church of San Lorenzo in Florence he seems to have been trying to design the side aisle bay to approximate a perfect central plan, which, continued as the perimeter of the church, would establish its basic and repetitive spatial module. One side of each side aisle bay is of course the nave arcade that is the seam between aisle and nave. Brunelleschi repeated the elements of that nave arcade as two other sides of the spatial unit, the arched portals that mark the seam between bays (figure 113). The fourth side of the spatial unit is the outside wall of the building, opposite the arcade. And this presents a difficulty, because it *is* a wall—a solid surface, not a void. Brunelleschi tried to echo the elements of the other three sides. He placed pilasters against the wall to echo the nave arcade columns, and above them an arch, all this in dark stonework, *pietra serena*. But how to echo above these pilasters the nave arcade impost blocks—the pieces that there surmount the columns? He seems to have decided that a continuous entablature above the pilasters would be the most appropriate transposition of the idea. But the decision brought its problems: on this side of the spatial unit only, the entablature sharply divides the arch above from a rectangular zone below it. So seemingly because of formal necessity, the fourth side of each side aisle bay at San Lorenzo is radically unlike the other three.

At Santo Spirito Brunelleschi brought all four sides of each such bay into near-congruence by, in a sense, getting rid of the troublesome wall. He made it a sequence of exedrae, whose outward billow creates for the fourth side of each bay a void much like those of the other three sides (figure 114); all sides of each bay can thus be almost identical. These self-congruent bays then circumnavigate the church. The effect is that the volume of Santo Spirito is everywhere edged by a cool stasis; the eye finds resolution and repetition wherever it looks; it comes easily to rest in the calm harmony of the repeated elements. How, then, do these studiously ordered architectural units offer the essential richness of complexity? One must necessarily move through the space, and as one does so, the *pietra serena* boundaries of these volumes continually shift in their relationship to one another. (The experience can be suggested but

113
Filippo Brunelleschi,
San Lorenzo, Florence,
1421–60. A side aisle
bay as seen from the
opposite nave arcade.

114
Filippo Brunelleschi,
Santo Spirito,
Florence, 1436–82.
A side aisle bay
as seen from the
opposite nave arcade.

115
Santo Spirito.
A view toward the
crossing from the
south side aisle.

of course not really simulated by a still photo such as figure 115.) The beauty of Santo Spirito, at least for me, lies in the tension between these crisp static individual units of space and the fluid, infinitely changing relationships between them that are a consequence of human movement.

Complex Order as a Function of Memory

The Finnish architect Alvar Aalto in the early 1930s designed a library for the town of Viipuri: one of its public spaces is a small auditorium with an exquisitely undulating wood ceiling. The exterior wall of the auditorium consists of generous sheets of full-height glazing through which the ceiling can be seen from the exterior. And of course when, after entry and after traversing other rooms and corridors, one enters the auditorium, the ceiling is again visible, just as it was announced from the exterior. But this is not another version of the experience of the Pazzi Chapel. The Viipuri library does not reiterate a motif in one or several permutations; the auditorium ceiling is simply seen from two vantage points, one exterior and one interior.

More important, and again unlike the Pazzi Chapel, it does not continuously present the motif or a permutation of it to view. On the contrary, the theme of the ceiling cannot be seen during the journey from entry to auditorium. One must remember it as one moves through intervening and not directly reiterative spaces.

Sir Edwin Lutyens's houses are remarkably good illustrations of such a dependence on memory through discontinuous experience, but at a higher level of thematic abstraction. Little Thakeham in Sussex, of 1902, is typical. The house is approached along a path through a completely symmetrical garden and is entered on the axis of an equally symmetrical facade (figure 116). But once inside, one meets a blank wall. To move farther into the house, one has to find an opening well off axis, to the right on the wall opposite the entry. This leads to a small hallway. On the right is a stair; at left are two doorways that open to the main living hall. On entering this living hall, one sees on the left a wall that appears symmetrically organized around a fireplace; opposite is the wall whose windows overlook the southern garden. The dominant window in this garden wall is a half-circular bay whose arc falls tangent to the doorway wall through which we entered the room (figures 116, 117); so the window bay is markedly asymmetrical with regard to the living hall and its centered fireplace opposite. And yet the wall with doorways through which we entered the living hall extends to only about five-eighths of the room's height (figure 117); the ceiling continues uninterrupted across living hall and stair. With regard to this ceiling in its entirety the semicircular window bay falls exactly on centerline. This window bay then is on the centerline of the house; it is therefore the central feature of the garden facade and is also on axis with the entry facade that was the first experience of this complex journey (figure 116). This is not the only such sequence. The doorway through which we entered the living hall occurs in the wall that is five-eighths the room's height (figure 117). That wall contains a second doorway symmetrically located: the two seem a matched pair. But as can be seen on the plan (figure 116), they play utterly different roles in the organization of the house. The one nearest the garden wall determines an axis around which rooms at the eastern and western ends of the house are symmetrically organized. Their symmetry in turn can be discovered only by moving toward and into them, and apprehension of their relationship to one another is discontinuous because interrupted by the living hall in which their axis is largely ignored.

Although one can understand these relationships, as at the Pazzi Chapel, only by moving from one space to another over time, here, unlike the Pazzi Chapel, no two contiguous spaces are permutations of the same order. Lutyens reiterated the first-postulated order dis-

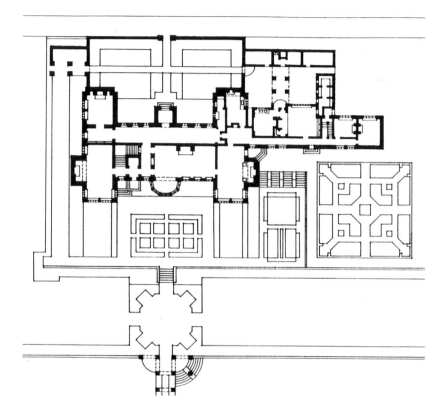

116
Sir Edwin Lutyens,
Little Thakeham,
Sussex, 1902. Plan:
entry is at top, the
garden at bottom;
the living hall is
at far center with
its "symmetrical"
fireplace and
"asymmetrical" bay
window. "East" and
"west" rooms are
to right and left in
this main block.

continuously, interrupting it with spaces whose order in each case differs from that of the immediately preceding space. The sequence of ordered relationships, therefore, is not evident in movement from one space to its immediate neighbor, and it cannot be understood by studying either the plan or the elevations in isolation. The same analysis would apply to Lutyens's Heathcote of 1906 near Ilkley in Yorkshire: one enters at the center of a symmetrical facade to find oneself in an almost symmetrical vestibule whose centerline of symmetry differs utterly from that of the external facade. Ednaston Manor of 1912–13, in Derbyshire, offers a similar instance, as do many of Lutyens's other houses.

Apparently we have a considerable ability to memorize such discontinuous orders. For all the complex discontinuities of Lutyens's work I expect just about everyone who moves through the spaces of Little Thakeham perceives, consciously or subconsciously, that its eastern and western rooms are symmetrical about a common axis, and that the semicircular bay of the living room, seen from the back garden, is on axis with the entry facade. I expect too

117
Little Thakeham.
The living hall, looking
toward the wall that
gives entry to the
space. At left is
the far jamb of the
semicircular bay
window that lies on
axis with the entry
and garden facades
(© Country Life
Picture Library).

that just about everyone, consciously or subconsciously, finds some degree of delight in these perceptions. It is easy to argue that this enjoyment too had an early usefulness: retention of the visual features, the sounds, even the rhythms, of the spaces through which we moved would have been significantly helpful in maintaining orientation in those resource-rich but complex early settings we sought and enjoyed. The process, after all, is fundamental to our enjoyment of music or dance: the thematic melody, or chord, or step, must linger in the mind because it vanishes from the senses with its very postulation.

And so it is with Louis Kahn's library for Phillips Exeter Academy of 1972 (figure 118). The facades are utterly repetitive, north like south like east like west, with brick piers in unbroken rhythm. (But the piers diminish in width with each ascending floor, and we are subtly drawn to the realization that the diminution is caused by inclined brickwork that at each floor creates a flat arch over each window [figure 119]. But is the arch flat? The eye tenuously perceives that it may not be, may escape being so by the slightest curvature. How can the eye measure

118
Louis Kahn, Library,
Phillips Exeter
Academy, Exeter,
New Hampshire, 1972
(© The Kahn
Collection, The
Architectural Archives
of the University of
Pennsylvania).

it? Our perception of straight lines, circles, even squares, is amazingly accurate: with experience we rapidly perceive irregularities of very small magnitude. Apparently such accuracy is possible because of the rapid scanning of the eye. At something like a hundred oscillations per second it moves along a line like a machine tool whose accuracy depends on the geometry, not of its edge, but of its movement.[31] So we perceive that the arches are slightly curved, not exactly flat—but so slightly curved that the eye keeps returning, attempting to assign them to one of two categories, each time reaching a conclusion so tenuous as to need continual rechecking.)

119
Library, Phillips
Exeter Academy.
Exterior detail (© The
Kahn Collection,
The Architectural
Archives of the
University of
Pennsylvania).

The exterior, then, is ordered but complex, but one thing is plain: it is symmetrical on each of its identical sides. So we expect to enter on axis. But that is where we cannot enter. How do we get in? A continuous colonnade edges the ground floor, a cloister turned inside out, but there are no clues to tell us where in its circumference an actual door exists. Exploration reveals an entry at the one place where the cloister is glazed. There we enter a vestibule and, moving forward, find a stair, or rather two curved runs of stairs (figure 120). These also cannot be ascended on the building's centerline. At this point in the experience we have lost contact with the building's basic order. We ascend on a curved and displaced path (figure 121) — and at the top of either stair reencounter, as in a Lutyens house, the building's centerline. At that point we see, in axial view, a great symmetrical central volume (figure 122), extending from the floor on which we stand to the very top of the building. Through exploration we have wandered the cloister, found the door, ascended, off axis, curvilinearly, a full floor, to rediscover the building's symmetry and centrality.

This volume seems insistently cubic. But it is not a cube, and none of its sides is a square. Our perception of a square may be related to our perception of a straight line; perhaps we divide the right angle of the corner rather neatly in half, and project the resultant bisecting line to intersect, or fail to intersect, the opposite corner; this at least is the process of which I am dimly aware when I try to judge squareness. In this regard, in the upper reaches of this space,

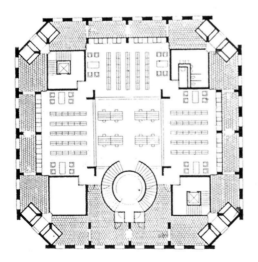
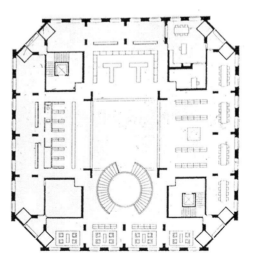

120
Library, Phillips
Exeter Academy.
Plans: entry floor left;
main floor right.

127

121
Library, Phillips Exeter
Academy. The stair
(© The Kahn
Collection, The
Architectural Archives
of the University
of Pennsylvania).

122
Library, Phillips Exeter
Academy. The central
volume (© The Kahn
Collection, The
Architectural Archives
of the University of
Pennsylvania).

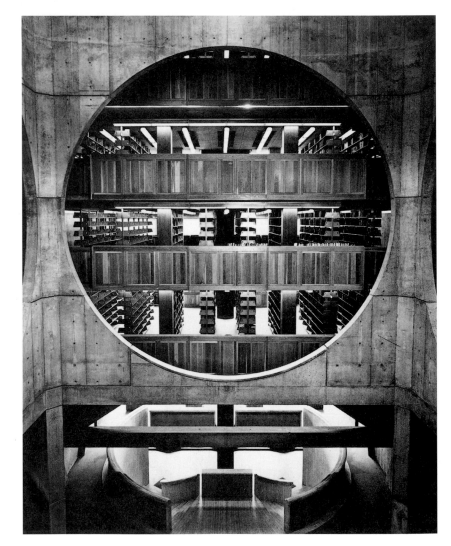

123
Library, Phillips Exeter
Academy. Looking
upward in the central
volume (© The Kahn
Collection, The
Architectural Archives
of the University of
Pennsylvania).

Kahn helps us; two enormous beams trace the diagonals, clarifying and confirming that the space is square in plan (figure 123). Square in elevation too, because those assertive circles of the walls (see figure 122), which the eye perceives to be as wide as they are high, lead to the conclusion that the walls they puncture must have the same property. Yet the conclusion is wrong, as the eye soon tells us; margins at top and bottom are not the same as those at the sides, and the whole set of relationships starts a full story above the floor on which we stand anyway; so the space as a whole cannot possibly be cubic. And in all this central space no allusionistic detail offers respite from an elemental order that is not elemental at all.

Finally, an example of dynamic and discontinous complex order that recalls some other matters too: a recent house in Sun Valley by Arne Bystrom. The exterior (figure 124) attempts to establish an order with the site: the roof slopes are the angles of repose of the landscape geology; the striated concrete below and the trunk-and-branches wood structure above are analogous to the forested rock of the mountains. When we move inside (figure 125), the order reappears, or a new version of it: the concrete striations are filled with color; the branchings

124
Arne Bystrom, a house
in Sun Valley, Idaho,
1996. Exterior detail
(© Arne Bystrom).

125
A house in Sun Valley.
The interior: complex
order, prospect and
refuge, and enticement
(© Arne Bystrom).

of the trees remain, but without the branches. The near part of the space offers interior refuge at left, prospect at right; above in the distance each of a multiplicity of secondary refuges enticingly reveals and conceals information-rich bits of itself.

So complex order is a characteristic of a number of settings that have attracted many different people over a long period of time. Designed as we are to take pleasure in categorizing and differentiating, we find that complex order in our surroundings rewards our innate mental attentions. It can be considered in a single space — in the composition both of the solids that bound it and of the resultant voids — and in sequences of spaces, groups of buildings, and buildings and their sites. It can reveal itself from a single vantage point, but also through movement from space to space over time; it can draw on memory to hold its patterns and relationships through discontinuous presentation. In its general sense it is a characteristic shared with many other arts. When it depends on movement and therefore involves time, it has especially interesting associations with dance and music. When it depends on memory, it has still more associations with music: themes, architectural and musical, are necessarily stored in the mind as data for returning reference. Ancient analogies between architecture and music may have a deep justification in the similar processes and pleasures of the human mind.

What are the limits, if any, of complex order as an element of architectural appeal? Is there an optimal degree of complexity, an optimal degree of order? Psychologists testing preferences in natural scenes find that increased complexity results in increased appeal, but only to a point, beyond which further increases diminish the appeal.[32] Here the arts, architecture included, may have something to contribute to the discourse. To my knowledge the order-complexity duality has never been tested *as a duality*; that is, high levels of complexity have not been tested for preference when accompanied by high degrees of order. Yet that is how they occur in the arts — which have expressed for twenty millennia and more our interest in the duality. The arts offer a reason to think that when order and complexity are linked, there may be no limit to the preferred degree of either. It is hard for me to imagine greater complexity than is found in, for example, a Chopin scherzo (op. 39, no. 3, perhaps), or a Gothic cathedral (Exeter, say, as in figure 91), yet each has a very high degree of order as well — and each rates very well in appeal if we look to its endurance in both critical and lay appreciation. Perhaps one function of the arts, architecture included, is to provide a sensory experience of complex order unparalleled in nature in either richness or extent, unique to products of human creativity.

The Problem of Accessibility

Both the order and the complexity must be made known; the audience must somehow get both parts of the message. In the examples I have cited, getting both parts of the message is ensured by making both openly accessible to the eye. This may seem so obvious as to need no saying. Yet there are cases in which order and complexity, though they exist, are in some respects not visible and depend instead, at least in part, on a cognitive knowledge of their presence. The thirteenth-century west towers of Laon cathedral (figure 126) are such a case. Their order is evident to the most casual eye: attenuated cylinders and prisms of masonry repeat in similar dimensions; proportions of openings in the masonry are roughly repetitive; the masonry itself is monochromatic.[33] There is to an equally casual eye some considerable sense of complexity as well: the plan of each ascending story is plainly not that of the story below; the balustrade at the top repeats established themes at radically different size; and there are

126
Laon cathedral.
The north tower of
the west facade.

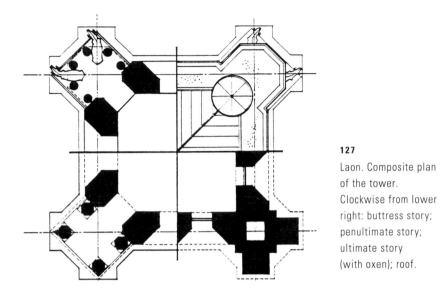

127

Laon. Composite plan
of the tower.
Clockwise from lower
right: buttress story;
penultimate story;
ultimate story
(with oxen); roof.

the unexpected animals in the upper porches, oxen whose heads seem turned every which way. Apparently the eye is satisfied; many people over a long period of time have liked these towers. But a more complete grasp of the ordered complexity here may depend on cognitive study of a series of abstractions, the plan sections through the various stories (figure 127).

The primary plan figure is the square formed by the imaginary centerlines of the buttresses. The plan of the story above the buttresses, the penultimate story, is determined by assigning one-third of the side of that buttress-centerline square as half the diagonal of smaller squares perched diagonally at the four corners; these are the empty porches at the corner of figure 126. Above, the octagonal porches of the ultimate story result from nipping off the corners of the porch geometries below; the oxen look out from the resultant octagons. And to bring everything to a nice closure, the centerlines of these oxen fall, as they must, on the buttress centerlines that started everything, while a closer look reveals that all the heads of the oxen are turned at forty-five degrees, the rotation that generated the porches at both levels. There are other such relationships in these towers, in elevation as well as plan: the height of the penultimate story, for example, is equal to the side of the original generating square. But perhaps enough has been cited to make the point that an understanding of some elements of these towers may depend on cognitive consideration. The *enjoyment* of the order and complexity remains innate — so much so that it is difficult to understand how it could be otherwise — but a full awareness that such order and complexity *exist* may depend on cognitive intervention.

Yet in the case of the towers of Laon I admit that I am not entirely sure, and do not know whether it is possible to be sure, that these relationships can be understood only by cognitive study of abstract representations—words or diagrams—or whether they may, in whole or in part, be intuitively apprehended. This is one instance among many of a gray area between intuitive and cognitive apprehension; hence my evasive "may" in the preceding paragraph. Nevertheless the towers of Laon introduce the point.

The mid twentieth century offers a less ambiguous illustration. Every architect trained in the United States and many other countries as well in the 1950s and 1960s was made aware of the corner detail of Mies van der Rohe's benchmark of Modernism, the Seagram Building of 1950 in New York. In a relationship visible only in a famous drawing (figure 128), the outer visible materials and shapes are seen to represent and express the inner steel frame that, necessarily hidden by fireproofing, nevertheless is the building's essential structure. Those who have studied this and other drawings understand the building to possess, behind its outer and evident order, this hidden complexity of relationships. So understood, the building can satisfy the aesthetic requisite of conjoined order and complexity. But while the order has been evident to all who look at the building, the complexity that has made it an icon to the initiated is apparent nowhere except in the drawing. It is not visible in the finished building, nor for that matter was it visible, as drawings represented it, even during the building's construction. Therefore full aesthetic enjoyment has depended on cognitive knowledge of an abstract diagram of the building's features rather than on features directly apprehended in the building itself. Those familiar with the building have always admired it, seeing it as an elegant il-

128
Ludwig Mies van der
Rohe and Philip
Johnson, the Seagram
Building, New York,
1950. Corner detail.

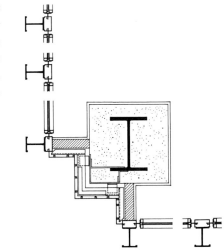

129
The Seagram Building.

lustration of Mies's dictum that "less is more." But it and its progeny have been less convincing to those who must depend on what is actually seen in situ, and who see there an obvious order but not enough complexity to reward attention (figure 129). From such a standpoint Robert Venturi is able to find some agreement with his comment that "less is a bore."[34]

A good bit of architecture since the last days of Modernism has had the opposite problem: although complexity has been obvious enough, order has eluded the eye. Many authors of recent buildings must have thought too that there might be a problem in that area; certainly it has been the fashion in recent years to accompany architectural projects, built and unbuilt, by lengthy — often very lengthy — verbal explanations of the ordering concepts they are meant to embody.[35]

Having It Both Ways

No good purpose is served by discarding exciting and fruitful growth that derives from speculation at a considerable level of cognitive abstraction; this book is in its way just such a speculation. But architecture is also a public art, and its qualities, or at least some of them, ought to be accessible to lay apprehension as well. Can we have it both ways?

I return to a comment by Nicholas Humphrey quoted early in this chapter: "Human babies who have been made familiar with a particular 'abstract' visual pattern take pleasure in seeing new patterns which are minor transformations of the original. . . . [but are not] attracted to stimuli which are wholly unrelated to what they have already seen."[36] He then cites Pavlov's observations of a similar behavior common to the adult world: "If we consider collecting in all its variations, it is impossible not to be struck with the fact that on account of this passion there are accumulated often completely trivial and worthless things, which represent absolutely no value from any point of view other than the gratification of the propensity to collect."

It is possible to extend the analogy to say that in the case of the Piazza San Marco, for example, we engage ourselves in "collecting" buildings with deeply shadowed arcades, wide and narrow arches, heavy superstructure, and elaborate skyline. And as we add to our collection different examples of this "thing," each a little different from the last, we experience pleasure. So too with the nave of Exeter: in each bay we build a collection of bundles of lines, each of about the same size but bearing a slightly different relationship to its neighbor, and of slightly different detail and coloration; then as we move from bay to bay we add to the collection by observing component elements that continually differ. By extending this argument a little we gain an insight into the value of creativity. For as we move through life, we find satisfaction in discovering new and different material for our collections, things related to earlier experiences but also in some way novel; conversely we are disappointed when we encounter an entirely familiar example — already, in a sense, in the collection. Thus we find stimulation in Michelangelo's *David*, which adds something — a great deal — to our mental file entitled "Human Figure." Although subsequently we may be disappointed by endless replicas of *David*, our interest is renewed by Rodin's *Burghers of Calais*; it belongs in the mental collection that already contains *David*, but it adds variations that seize our attention. So does a representation of the human figure by Edvard Munch or Paul Klee. Having heard a polonaise performed by Arthur Rubinstein, we add to our collection a new interpretation when Vladimir Ashkenazy sits down at the keyboard.

The professional artist — poet, sculptor, architect, musician, painter — is understandably intensely involved in a continually growing cognitive sophistication. In a time of rapidly developing ideas, however, this cognitive sophistication increasingly exceeds the grasp of a non-specialist audience. The cognitive sophistication cannot and should not be set aside; it is the key to rich progress. But must it be exclusive? Might we not rediscover, and reinclude, a linkage to the collecting needs of a broader audience in the affective values of the artifact? The problem is there in all the arts, but it is crucial to address it in architecture, which has unavoidable large-scale, long-term public dimensions.

The towers of Laon suggest an approach. They were designed to represent some quite sophisticated and abstract thinking of their time: preoccupations with the metaphysical meanings of geometry; with the symbolism of light, whose admission was made possible with mastery of a skeletal armature of stone; and with an architecture subconsciously cousin to the scholastic unity that, like Aquinas's *Summa*, could accept and reconcile an infinite variety. These abstract issues of the building's form, however, were far beyond the layperson of the time — probably they are outside the realm of many knowledgeable modern tourists, for that matter. Yet these towers also present characteristics of immediate and visible delight. They have it both ways: they add to one observer's collection at a sophisticated cognitive level, to another's at an immediately apparent affective level. I wonder, in fact, whether the combination, the having-it-both-ways, might not be a useful general characteristic of long-term architectural success. The building that works only on the level of intuitive appeal is unlikely to reward further cognitive examination, while the one whose interest depends largely on cognitive explication will be further explored only by the initiated few. The building rich in both dimensions has the chance of garnering many audiences and extended interest.

SOME CLOSING
COMMENTS

THIS BOOK HAS EXPLORED THE POSSIBILITY that some of our responses to architecture may originate in the innate behaviors of our distant ancestors.

But few examples in this book are vernacular; few other than the cave and grove themselves are of really early date. Why? If our fondness for the characteristics described herein has been with us on a widespread basis more or less from the beginning, one would expect a selection of examples weighted as much toward the very early and the vernacular as toward professionally designed work of recent centuries and decades. But early and vernacular work are up against some handicaps. Although the refuge aspect of a building, at least in the barest sense, must have been common enough from the beginning—from say, the time of the Dartmoor stone hut or the caves of ancient time—the offering of prospect is a different matter. A prospect that really counts demands a broad arc of view and a considerable reach of vista. These can sometimes be found in the primordial habitat—the communal spaces of Spruce Tree House at Mesa Verde are an extreme example. But when one gets to a building—that Dartmoor hut, again, or individual structures at Spruce Tree House—opening a wide arc of view presents structural problems. Furthermore, one basic reason for buildings is to exclude weather, and until glass began to be produced in quantity, a wide arc of view meant problems on that score too. So we find little in the way of generous prospect in early buildings—until the development of reasonable means for making a lot of glass and managing, one way or another, an appreciable clear span. I have also emphasized the appeal of prospect and refuge at a hierarchically smaller scale on the interior of the building. Among other things, interior prospect and refuge depend on significant differences in ceiling height. This dependence of course again takes us out of the realm of the Dartmoor hut, and even out of that of much pre-twentieth-century work. Before that time the typical modest or moderate house was multi-storied with a gable or hip roof. The undersurfaces of spaces above foreclosed significant height differences among rooms on the lower floor(s), while the ceiling under the crossties of the roof structure foreclosed significant differences on the top floor. Some exceptions come to mind. There is the typical English great hall in which the central space is indeed open to the roof, often with a two-story arrangement of smaller rooms at one or both ends; these rooms are therefore less than half the height of the hall, and those on the upper story look from a vantage point of refuge down toward the prospect of the great hall. But an additional requisite of interior refuge and prospect is contrast in light quantity, and no English great hall example of which I am aware has a markedly bright great hall, for reasons described just above.[1]

Likewise enticement demands enough spaces and solids to mask some relatively distant features, while the revealed parts of those distant features gain in drawing power as they present suggestions of complex order. These characteristics, earlier found in nature, are architecturally possible only in buildings of some size and some degree of spatial and formal accomplishment. Similar limitations apply to architectural peril: it can be developed only in the context of a dramatic site, or a building of considerable vertical dimension or generous interior volume.

The argument for the fundamental appeal of prospect and refuge, enticement, peril, and complex order, therefore, can be made theoretically, as governing our responses to settings consisting largely or entirely of natural materials; but when we transfer the argument to architecture, it cannot so easily be illustrated in early or vernacular examples. We have the paradoxical situation that our earliest elemental predilections have been capable of extensive architectural exploitation only in historical times.

And only in relatively modern times have we developed the possibility of realizing those innate predilections on a less-than-aristocratic budget. In earlier times buildings of generous volume and complex spatial and formal order, with high and low spaces, constrained and expansive spaces, light and dark spaces, perhaps on a dramatic site as well—such buildings were costly, very costly. In the last century or two new materials and methods have meant the achievement of such buildings at reasonable expense. Which, in turn, leads me to wonder whether these observations suggest a somewhat different interpretation of those earlier expensive buildings that, long famous in one way or another, have sometimes been portrayed as primarily symbols of power or wealth. Might it be that many of those buildings secure our attention not just by their evidence of power and wealth but also because such power and wealth have enabled them — some of them — to manifest characteristics we deeply like? If this is true, it means — perhaps — that many buildings that make the history books are simply buildings that through extra expenditure of time and money have succeeded in rewarding some quite fundamental interests of many people over a long period of time.

I said at the outset that this approach is not meant to be exclusive; it is also not comprehensive.

There is widespread belief that some design successes depend on proportion; certainly it has been a subject of architectural theory since Vitruvius. My approach in this book has few insights to offer on it. In considering Kahn's Phillips Exeter library as an instance of complex order, we can speculate that the rapid scanning movement of the eye enables it to evaluate straight lines, circles, and even squares. It may be too that our grasp of such settings is related to Sommerhoff's conditional expectancy: the identical angles and sides of a square, the continual unvarying deflection in the curve of a circle yield satisfaction because they repeat a familiarized condition. It may even be that our pleasure in the golden section is similarly based: we perceive side a of a rectangle to bear the same relationship to side b as b does to $a + b$, and so our expectation is fulfilled. But these are at best open questions, and the last example, for me at least, stretches credibility too far.[2] As for such questions as whether we can perceive in the spaces of Palladio's villas an embodiment of the mathematical relationships of sixteenth-century northern Italian music — maybe future work in physiology or psychobiology will demonstrate that such things happen and will tell us how; for now, I concede them incapable of analysis in this framework. (I have discussed some parallels between seeing and hearing. It is tempting to draw further ones, but one soon runs up against the different principles that govern the eye and the ear. The eardrum, as a taut diaphragm, vibrates sympathetically to sound waves that mesh with one another mathematically; the eye, in contrast, functions physiologically as a mechanism of quite randomly distributed light-sensing rods and cones. The same analytical approach cannot apply. Many analogies between music and architecture have been suggested, over many centuries — I have suggested some in these pages. But when we begin to talk about the physiological mechanisms of sensory perception, the audial and the visual part company.)

It cannot reasonably be denied that color matters in our innate perceptions, so much so that the effect of many of the illustrations in this book would be influenced by their reproduction in color. Some things can be said about color in a psychobiological interpretation. For example, blues and greens are generally regarded as restful, since both were ubiquitous in our early habitation, the arboreal or savanna setting with its supportive lakes and rivers. They stood for shelter, water, and vegetable — and to some extent animal — food sources. "The lushness of the setting and the color of the sky . . . are known to influence response to landscapes."[3] Perhaps this is why "Tarahumara speakers of Northern Mexico name all of green and blue with one term."[4] Animals programmed to pay attention to a flickering red image, moreover, are therefore programmed to notice and respect fire and thus to survive; hence many of the usual associations of red — red lights, red flags, and so forth — as an attention-commanding color for animals, including ourselves. (Carl Sagan ignores this aspect of red but notes that red, as the color of blood, may be associated with injury and therefore danger; this view also rings true to me. He mentions too that red is the color of the "down" signal in elevator direction lights: "Our arboreal ancestors had to be very careful of down"[5] — but I think he overreaches here; the "down" signal on elevators is by no means universally red.) And given our predilection for order, it may well be that similar degrees of saturation in the various colors of a scene, or similarities of value, or permutations of the same hue arouse in us some satisfying sense of ordered relationships, a confirmation of expectancies. We can in fact analyze our feelings when we are presented with such color relationships as being roughly these. But such an analysis is fairly obvious, and beyond it there seems to be, at present, no clear chain of reasoning about color from a survival-advantage perspective.

I have not mentioned our relationship to tools. It seems certain that in an evolutionary sense we were selected for the unique degree to which we have recognized potential tools in the raw material of the world around us and have exploited these to extend our abilities. This supposition is supported by observations that chimpanzees recognize, modify, and use tools. It is also supported by the ubiquitous tendency for babies to grab things they can grab and shortly thereafter to convert this intuition into simple tool use. We have also been selected for our ability to analyze the efficiency and manufacture of tools, and not only in technologically advanced stages of our development: the early tribe whose tool-manufacturing intuitions produced the most effective and efficiently made spearhead would have had an advantage in combat with the woolly mammoth — and with neighboring woolly mammoth hunters too, for that matter. Further, since the relationship between early innate predilections, survival advantage, and pleasure has now been extensively argued, it seems reasonable to postulate that we like to recognize, make, use, and develop tools. Our satisfaction at inserting the peg in the tenon or dropping the timber into the sockets of the ancient portal offers everyday evidence of our delight in the obviously workable device. So far so good. But by what intuitions can we be thought to have recognized and developed tools? Does this process demand some innate sensitivity to the suggestions made by the tool itself, some ability to "read" its operative characteristics, its potential for development, its mode of effectuation? To suppose that it does seems, at a theoretical level, eminently reasonable. From this supposition should also follow the pleasure we derive from "reading" the tool's character, mode of operation, and potential for development. In what can this "reading" consist? We now move into a realm of more tenuous speculation. But let us proceed, nevertheless, for the moment. We might hypothesize that such features as graspability, portability, and readiness or ease of employment must be evident to our innate understanding, and that we find pleasure in such understanding. If this hypothesis holds, then the features, or some features, of tools must be "eloquent"—capable of telling us, in a sense, how they work or how they might be put to work.

And so it should be that as buildings present to us characteristics similar to those of tools to which we are attuned, we extend to those buildings the same pleasure response. Here may be the basis for our interest in and enjoyment of tectonic expression. What buildings suggest themselves as germane examples? Barns? Only as they bear tool-suggesting features, and my guess is that they do not, or do so only in small ways; if they have an innate appeal, its basis may lie elsewhere—in our useful tendency to domesticate animals, for example. We might, in contrast, usefully examine the columns of the Greek temple, or the ribs of the Gothic cathedral, for tool-suggesting and pleasure-generating characteristics. But if architecture can indeed include tool-suggestions and tool-pleasures, the richest examples surely lie in the present and the very recent past, in the work of architects such as Renzo Piano, Richard Rogers, Philip Cox, and Glenn Murcutt; or the work of Arne Bystrom, Kazunari Sakamoto, and Eric Owen Moss, illustrated in figures 8, 124, 125, 10, 76, and 77.

I have not pursued the subject of tool-predilections and their relationship to tectonics, however, because I have tried to develop in this book issues for which there is some empirical support—not proof, but support. And tool recognition and development as aspects of our psychobiological predilections resist empirical examination, in part because the variables are frustratingly difficult to isolate for testing. It might be thought, for instance, that one could show a neutral audience slides of architecture, automobiles, cameras, kitchen equipment, whatever, some examples of which we postulate are "eloquent" in revealing their purpose and mode of operation, and others that we postulate are "mute." We might think a manual typewriter more eloquent in this sense than a word processor, since the typewriter's mechanisms and movements that create the letter on the sheet of paper are apparent to the eye, while the word processor gives no visual clue to the relation between depressing a key and the appearance of something on the screen. If we wished to support our speculations, we would hope that some randomly selected group of Homo sapiens would prefer the "eloquent" typewriter over the "mute" word processor. But here lies one instance of a general problem, because the choice is likely to be made for reasons unrelated to our focus. The typewriter might be picked for nostalgia, for example, or — a much more likely outcome — the word processor might be chosen for its cognitively known overwhelmingly superior efficiency. If we are to hope for a defensible empirical complement to the theoretical argument on this issue, then, the task is going to need sophisticated guidance.

I ventured at the outset that this inquiry would not lead to quantifiable objectivity, and I have kept my word. I have not described means by which one can determine how much refuge is correct in a given circumstance for a given observer, or how to measure the amount of enticement necessary to entice. I doubt that such means exist. In a measure-oriented age this may seem a mortal flaw in this approach, especially as it purports to establish links between aesthetics and the natural sciences. But such an approach depends on a cognizance of the infinite small individual differences that in any case demand elasticity of specification. Equally important, the very concept of the archetype as explored here necessitates, both theoretically and operationally, accepting inexactness in any particular manifestation, as I noted in Chapter 1 and emphasize here again. To these considerations must be added the architectural permutations, modifications, and developments that ought to occur, and ought to be welcomed, in the continuing creative evolution of the field. It follows that in the approach to architectural experience described here, or any workable future development of it, large matters of judgment and approximation are going to remain and should remain. I intend what I put forward here, not as a numerically quantifiable prescription, but rather as a reasonably coordinated and integrated framework, with a reasonably defined and understandable terminology, a reasonably consistent theoretical basis, and a reasonable degree of empirical support, that might serve the exercise of critical and creative judgment.

We now reach the point beyond caveats and reservations where something positive can be claimed. We are left with six characteristics: the necessarily complementary prospect and refuge; the more or less autonomous enticement and peril; and the necessarily coexistant order and complexity. These characteristics are intrinsic to the configuring of architectural space; the locations, sizes, patterns, and rhythms of the solids that bound and describe it; the light that illuminates it or is withheld from it; and the temporal dimension of movement through it—all regarded from the point of view of some of Homo sapiens's fundamental choices in these matters.

Conditions of refuge and prospect, keys to our appropriate habitation, essentially depend on spatial dimensions, light, and view. Refuge is spatial circumscription, darkness, and limited view; prospect is spatial openness, brightness, and extended view. These characteristics, necessarily juxtaposed, have let us see without being seen; they have let us hide in safety and forage in safety. Transferred to architecture, these characteristics can be developed in complex hierarchical sequences. They can be chosen and emphasized in the site itself, in the exterior characteristics of the building, and in the relationship between the building's features and those of the site. They can also be developed at smaller scale as interior characteristics in what I have called a nested hierarchy, as in almost any house by Wright or Botta. In both exterior and interior they can be deployed in an array sufficiently rich to give the occupant of the space a range of conditions so that the surroundings can suit even momentary emotional states.

The exploratory stimulus of enticement is also determined by relative containment and openness, darkness and light. It differs from the refuge-prospect condition in suggesting further information withheld from immediate view by the intervention of intermittent solids or, in rare cases, atmosphere or light itself. Such a stimulus is most compelling when there is a sense that exploration can be undertaken in safety, thus the typical enticement characteristic of movement from a darker to a brighter zone. Exploration is also related to conditions of peril, ubiquitous in the skyscraper city and latent in modern materials and spatial possibilities.

Complex order, most obviously a matter of the solid material of architecture, can also be experienced in the relationship of spaces to one another. And in terms of both the solids and the spaces, it can be experienced dynamically, and discontinuously, by means of movement over time.

As we inhabit and use buildings, these terms in themselves may help us to describe, evaluate, and choose especially satisfying spaces. More important, they may help us to describe, evaluate, and choose satisfying sequences and varieties of spaces that offer opportunities for many different experiences. We can use these terms for these purposes whether or not their theoretical basis in survival advantage is substantiated or modified in the future. They are useful terms for evaluating individual preferences without regard to any universality they may or may not claim.

So much for their value in lay usage. Their value to the professional differs somewhat. For the designer their usefulness will depend on the role they may play in the design of a building. In particular, complex order will play a role that is fundamentally different from that of refuge and prospect, enticement, and peril.

Let us consider, first of all, the design process as it relates to order and complexity (a separation of the two terms in this case will make the discussion easier). As the designer develops an architectural project, the complexities are usually all too obvious. The struggle lies in discovering or devising an appropriate order that will inform and orchestrate those complexities and perhaps suggest others. Such an order may emerge only after long weeks, months, occasionally even years of concentration, sketching, talking, discarding; its last details may be resolved only as the building nears completion. The designer struggling toward order can seek help by returning to some basic considerations: the pragmatic uses intended for the building; the climate; the site; technically feasible ways of doing things; appropriate ways of doing things. The order will emerge too from the designer's own ways of doing things, conscious or subconscious though these be. But these guides and constraints are rarely enough. For further help the designer usually constructs or brings to the task another device: a metaphorical or expressive intention, a stance or position, more or less clearly worked out and stated, that may derive from, and certainly will relate to, some larger external reference or purpose. This position is likely to change only modestly from project to project in the work of any designer; it will be central to that designer's individuality. It will differ more significantly from one designer to another, but—at least in the past, and probably in the present too—some commonalities in ways of forming solutions will link contemporaneous designers with one another.

Because this aspect of the design process—the derivation of a complex order—is both difficult and richly rewarding, it accounts for much of the verbiage of architectural discourse, through which the most interesting problems of the profession are redefined, individual positions are declared and disputed, and the intellectual foundation for the architectural profession evolves.

But can the complex orders of the resultant built work be perceived in some way by those who are not part of the generative discourse? The orders and complexities of some recent work have depended on an extensive familiarity with some highly involved explication; and here lies a problem. For although "people should be enticed by the prospect of updating and extending their cognitive maps. . . . they cannot stray too far from the familiar, lest they be caught in a situation in which they are helpless because they lack the necessary knowledge."[6] When intellectual discourse is rapidly advancing in sophistication, this observation may be worth keeping in mind; in public architecture it may even constitute something of an obligation. If buildings are to appeal by virtue of that complex order common to all the arts, they must convey it to the observer in some way. For the lay observer the simplest and often the only access to complex order is by way of features openly visible to the eye; but even for the initiated such access may be important in establishing an immediate, intuitive, and fundamental attraction. It seems to follow, then, that from just about any point of view, some element of the complex order of an architectural work ought to be substantially accessible to the eye, in addition to any cognitive content accessible through sophisticated discourse. There is no reason why the two realms should be mutually exclusive. I think again of the Gothic. Although it pursued some highly cognitive theoretical purposes, its physical entity is rich in material to engage the eye's discovery.

Prospect, refuge, enticement, and peril occupy a somewhat different position: they are, in a sense, nested within the search for a complex order. Any architectural project worth doing entails, of necessity, decisions about the three dimensions of its spaces, the opening or closing of spaces to one another, the presence and absence of transparent and opaque bounding surfaces, the availability, location, and character of vistas, the composition of paths of movement. Such decisions must be made in configuring the essential constituent material—the solids and the spaces—of any architecture. Concepts of prospect and refuge, enticement, and peril are simply ways of providing a certain kind of information for such decisions.

It is worth emphasizing here that in the professional creative context the theoretical foundation of these concepts can be highly useful. For that theoretical foundation enables us to discuss these concepts in terms of our emerging understanding of deep-seated and widely shared human responses to large and small, light and dark, hidden and revealed, safe and dangerous, ordered and complex. Thus that theoretical foundation makes some of our emotional responses to architecture paradoxically amenable to rational analysis. It can help to shape fruitful questions for such analysis; it can provide a road map for further development and creative application of the informing concepts. And as these concepts may be developed, modified, and refined by such means, they ought, then, to hold the promise of an architecture of widespread pleasure.

That last sentence—and this entire book—reveal the assumption that the concepts described and illustrated here can indeed be creatively applied and developed. Can they? A

Darwinian point of view toward human activities often seems to engender anxiety about words like "individuality" and "creativity"; if, after all, our seemingly individual choices and actions, likes and dislikes, are just instances of innate behaviors selected over aeons by the harsh culling of survival, where does this leave notions of human choice, of individuality, of creativity? It seems to me that it leaves them alive and in quite good health. There is a Darwinian argument—I briefly outlined it in Chapter 4—for the creation and performance of music: the pleasure we find in hearing a piece by, say, Paul Simon, and the pleasure we assume he found in composing it, are versions of a pleasure that has been useful—essential—to our managing in this world, and so Simon's music is a manifestation of a universal and, in a way, a predestined behavior. But that argument does not mean that any particular piece by Simon, or the entire corpus of his work, is in any sense inevitable in that form. It is a creative and individual manifestation of a general predilection. Furthermore, the discoveries we make as we hear a piece by Simon on any particular occasion are not only individual to ourselves but are unique to that moment. And just as in Simon's music the presence of a mathematical structure has directed rather than inhibited creativity, so too the concepts suggested here as bases for architectural judgment are foundations capable of yielding an infinite variety of superstructures. The very catholicity of examples cited in this book argues such an infinite creativity. And perhaps we can take some comfort too in the likelihood that we will always seek invention, novelty, a new variation on a theme, since, as I suggested in Chapter 4, our lust for the creative is itself an innate predilection.

There is another assumption that underpins this book, that human pleasure is a legitimate architectural purpose. Not everyone will agree with that assumption. Some would say that ours is a not a time of order, comfort, pleasure, reassurance; our work should express the clash and dissonance that are the true essence of our time. That is one way of looking at architectural purpose, and I would not necessarily quarrel with it; it faces the nature of our time with poignantly straightforward courage. But there are other respectable ways to contemplate a relationship between architecture and society. Gyorgy Kepes commented many years ago, during a visit to the University of Washington, that art of importance might not only concern itself with what a society is; it might also address what a society needs. Since, on examination, most times seem to have a dismal abundance of clash and dissonance, Kepes's observation may be useful. Certainly it has its exemplars: Chartres cathedral was built in an appallingly violent time, yet its sculptural program is free from any depiction of violence; Santo Spirito's tranquil spaces reside in a city torn by perpetual and bitter strife. But the issue may be moot in this present context. If evolutionary psychology is on solid ground, as a substantial, growing, and consistent body of evidence suggests, then pleasurable responses to certain characteristics of our surroundings are built into us in ways that transcend any immediate societal trends. The rejection of such characteristics is an unnecessary frustration, their provision an obvious satisfaction of predilections that lie within us all.

Some Introductory Comments

1. Stephen Kaplan. "Aesthetics, Affect, and Cognition," in *Environment and Behavior*, 19, no. 1 (Jan. 1987): 7.

2. See e.g. Roger Ulrich, "Aesthetic and Affective Response to Natural Environment," in *Behavior and the Natural Environment*, ed. I. Altman and J. F. Wohlwill, 85–125 (New York: Plenum, 1983).

3. That the images were selected for high visual quality of course raises the question of the criteria used to ascribe such quality. This book intends to develop some hypotheses in response to that question. But for immediate purposes the answer does not matter. The students in this case were simply trying to take a first step, to see whether some fabricated settings could compete with some natural settings, and they found that some could; Q.E.D.

4. And they have been: Mary Victoria Porter, in a master's thesis ("The Role of Spatial Quality and Familiarity in Determining Countryside Landscape Preference," University of Washington, 1987), finds similar responses in fieldwork among farmers in Whatcom County, Washington.

5. This point has troubled, even offended, some readers who are dedicated to the paramount importance of temporal and cultural differences. Although I do not deny the interest and importance of that point of view, I do not accept a rejection of this one, which offers another way of understanding, one that to many—see the epigraph to this book from Carl Sagan—has seemed and continues to seem a worthwhile and important complement to other ways of understanding ourselves and the world we have shaped. In this connection it may be worth mentioning that humanistic studies from at least the time of Thucydides have concerned themselves with things we have in common across time and space — and, by necessary inference, across cultures.

6. Gordon H. Orians and Judith H. Heerwagen, "Evolved Responses to Landscapes," in *The Adapted Mind*, ed. J. Barkow, L. Cosmides, and J. Toobey, 91 (Oxford: Oxford University Press, 1993). In fairness, however, Roger Ulrich ("Biophilia, Biophobia, and Natural Landscapes," in *The Biophilia Hypothesis*, ed. Stephen R. Kellert and Edward O. Wilson, 91 [Washington, D.C.: Island Press, 1993]) notes that

"whereas most studies have found that on-site ratings of settings that are static correlate highly with ratings of color slides, the validity issue has not been fully resolved."

1. The Aesthetics of Survival

1. Continuing skepticism, including the widely known but often not carefully read critiques of Stephen Jay Gould, is seriously addressed, point by point, in an ongoing literature. For a detailed up-to-date synopsis, see especially Daniel C. Dennett, *Darwin's Dangerous Idea* (New York: Touchstone, 1996).

2. Daniel Dennett, in *Darwin's Dangerous Idea* (New York: Touchstone, 1996), 290, quotes Darwin himself describing such a process: "Many species once formed never undergo any further change . . . ; and the periods, during which species have undergone modification, though long as measured by years, have probably been short in comparison with the periods during which they retain the same form." But my rereading of Darwin leads me more to the conclusion that he was thinking this matter through by putting various views on paper, as he seems to have done on many such issues.

3. The "instantaneous" position, impressively named "punctuated equilibrium," has, in my opinion, been especially overdramatized; see e.g. Richard Dawkins, *The Blind Watchmaker* (London: Longmans, 1986), 251: "What needs to be said now, loud and clear, is the truth: that the theory of punctuated equilibrium lies firmly within the neo-Darwinian synthesis. It always did. It will take time to undo the damage wrought by the overblown rhetoric, but it will be undone." For a balanced summary of the debate see Dennett, *Darwin's Dangerous Idea*, 263–312.

4. There are dramatic exceptions. Birds on isolated islands have rapidly evolved alternative beak structures when faced with rapidly changing food sources. The stimulus to such rapid change is the type of available food — those ill-equipped to eat the new nourishment die very quickly, as do their offspring if they manage to produce any. The rapidity of change also relates to generational time: when a species produces a generation or two a year, a hundred generations, and the selection processes of which they are record, pass by in a hurry. Presumably insects under like pressures could adapt with even greater speed.

5. Graham Greene, *The Power and the Glory* (London: Penguin, 1962), 12. Greene had a particular interest in this phenomenon; see e.g. *The Ministry of Fear* (London: Penguin, 1963), 88: "The impressions of childhood are ineffaceable."

6. I cite a case in my own life. My father was a painter and sculptor; in the Great Depression when I was small, we lived on a trickle of money from WPA projects; by the outbreak of World War II there was not even much of that. In those years I had two playmates whose families had a more comfortable income and were kind as well. I was occasionally invited for dinner and on several occasions was taken to a movie, the ultimate treat; those times and places were unusually happy ones. One playmate lived in a Gothic Revival mansion, the other in a house designed by Alden Dow, one of Frank Lloyd Wright's abler followers. Those houses retain in my mind an association with happiness. In my later career in architecture I have been most engaged by the Gothic and the work of Wright and have thought more than once that that is not accidental. It does, however, seem ineradicable.

7. This sounds Homo sapiens–directed, but other creatures seem to have degrees of enculturation too. And among Homo sapiens the meanings of enculturated elements are far from clear. The Greco-Roman orders seem an obvious case of shared meaning in many regions of the Western world, yet exactly what those orders mean is hard to discern. In a vague way they seem to stand for dignity, learning, perhaps institutional grandeur, but it is surprisingly hard to describe a more specific "meaning." In this context, George Hersey (*The Lost Meaning of Classical Architecture* [Cambridge, Mass.: MIT Press, 1988]) argues, to me convincingly, that meanings ascribed to these forms at the time of their original usage may be not only vastly different from the ones we infer but also, to us, in our circumstances, utterly inappropriate, perhaps even repugnant.

8. Carl Sagan and Ann Druyan, *Shadows of Forgotten Ancestors* (New York: Ballantine, 1992), 168. This is the famous "waggling dance" discovered by Karl von Frisch, a pioneer in this kind of study (see e.g. his *Bees: Their Vision, Chemical Senses, and Language* [Ithaca, N.Y.: Great Seal Books, 1950]). In that connection it should be mentioned that the waggling dance has a sophistication not mentioned in the text quoted. The deviation from the vertical of the path "danced" by the messenger bee establishes the horizontal angle from the sun necessary for flight to the food (and through a reading of polarized light the bees can establish this direction without seeing the sun directly). The speed at which the bee waggles communicates the distance to the food, but the relation between the danced frequency and the actual distance is exponentially scaled. And to be fair, it is an imperfect world: about twenty percent of the bees fail to get the message.

9. Sagan and Druyan, *Shadows of Forgotten Ancestors*, 376.

10. There is now a large body of material on this phenomenon in birds; see e.g. John Alcock, *Animal Behavior*, 6th ed. (Sunderland, Mass.: Sinauer, 1997).

11. Roger Ulrich, "Aesthetic and Affective Response to Natural Environment," in *Behavior and the Natural Environment*, ed. I. Altman and J. F. Wohlwill, 87 (New York: Plenum, 1983).

12. Human babies at the onset of crawling have been placed in cribs with glass panels in the mattress, revealing a surface apparently far below. Babies will not crawl across such a panel.

13. See e.g. Graham Richards, *Human Evolution* (London: Routledge and Kegan Paul, 1987), 132–204, and especially 150. Richards's work is a compendium; therefore the views presented are not his alone but purport to represent the range of viewpoints currently a part of serious discourse.

14. Carl Sagan, *The Dragons of Eden* (New York: Ballantine, 1977), 95.

15. Robert Wright, *The Moral Animal* (New York: Vintage, 1995), 44.

16. Design, in approximately this sense, though often with a different agenda, has been a part of Darwinian discourse from the beginning, so there is long-standing precedent for the term: see e.g. Dennett, *Darwin's Dangerous Idea*, 64ff. This view of behavior and motivation contrasts with our usual assumptions of the relationship between cause and beneficial effect as motivated by conscious or subconscious consideration of beneficial outcomes. The familiar assumed sequence is awareness of desired outcome, conscious or subconscious consideration of behaviors likely to obtain it, selection of a particular behavior, and enjoyment of the desired outcome. (Or if the outcome sought is not obtained, we reassess and try again.) Innate behaviors, however, are enacted without consideration of effect, often without

even awareness of effect, and natural selection determines the perpetuation of those whose results are beneficial. A particularly enjoyable discussion of the process as it selects for the trait of familial love is found in Wright, *The Moral Animal,* 158–60.

17. There is a considerable literature on this subject in the field of psychology. For a recent summarizing discussion see Robert MacLaury, "Prototypes Revisited," *Annual Review of Anthropology* 20 (1991): 55–74. See also Edward O. Wilson, "Biophilia and the Conservation Ethic," in *The Biophilia Hypothesis,* ed. Stephen R. Kellert and Edward O. Wilson, 34 (Washington, D.C.: Island Press, 1993). From a paragraph on this point one statement may suffice: "The slithering motion of an elongate form appears to be the key stimulus producing snake aversion."

18. Nicholas Humphrey, "Natural Aesthetics," in *Architecture for People,* ed. Byron Mikellides, 73 (London: Studio Vista, 1980), makes a similar point:

> If I were asked for a prescription for where architects and planners should go to learn their trade, it would be this: Go out to nature and learn from experience what natural structures men find beautiful, because it is among such structures that men's aesthetic sensitivity evolved. [But] if I seem to be arguing for an aesthetics of "naturalism" it is not the naive naturalism which would have each element mimic a natural object.

19. Michael Brill, in "Using Archetypes in the Design of 'Charged' Places," a paper written for the Horace W. S. Cleveland Fellowship of the landscape architecture program (University of Minnesota, 1989, 2), has made the same point in discussing fabricated surrogates for the natural world—"charged" places, as he calls them:

> People of many cultures and from many times have been stunned by the caves at Altamira and Lascaux, by Stonehenge and the Pyramids, and always will be. This happens on seeing them for the first time, and again. Because you don't have to be of the time or the culture to feel its power, it seems to be a special response, recurrent in a special place, that transcends boundaries of both time and of individual cultures. It acts as if it were a species-wide phenomenon, one experienced by all humans, everywhere. If so, it must have very ancient roots indeed.

20. Research in responses to natural settings has shown this to be true; see e.g. Roger Ulrich, "Biophilia, Biophobia, and Natural Landscapes," in *The Biophilia Hypothesis,* ed. Kellert and Wilson, 93:

> The pattern of findings that has emerged over the last two decades runs directly counter to the initial expectation of wide differences as a function of learning or experience-related variables. The overarching conclusion . . . is that similarities in responses to natural scenes usually far outweigh the differences across individuals, groups, and diverse European, North American, and Asian cultures.

21. Humphrey, "Natural Aesthetics" (as in n. 18).

22. John Dewey, *Art as Experience* (New York: Pentagon, 1934), 4, 13.

23. Gottfried Semper, *The Four Elements of Architecture and Other Writings*, trans. Harry Francis Mallgrave and Wolfgang Herrmann (Cambridge: Cambridge University Press, 1989), 102.

24. Michael Benedikt, *Deconstructing the Kimbell* (New York: Sites/Lumen, 1991), 48. Benedikt returns to this point several times in this book, always briefly, but his thoughts on the matter are provocative.

2. Finding a Good Home

1. Stephen Kaplan, "Aesthetics, Affect, and Cognition," *Environment and Behavior* 19, no. 1 (Jan. 1987): 3.

2. Roger Ulrich, in a talk given at the College of Architecture and Urban Planning, University of Washington, Dec. 6, 1990.

3. Edward O. Wilson, "Biophilia and the Conservation Ethic," in *The Biophilia Hypothesis*, ed. Stephen R. Kellert and Edward O. Wilson, 32 (Washington, D.C.: Island Press, 1993).

4. Roger Ulrich, "Biophilia, Biophobia, and Natural Landscapes," in *The Biophilia Hypothesis*, 73.

5. Ibid., 105–7.

6. Gordon H. Orians and Judith H. Heerwagen, "Evolved Responses to Landscapes," in *The Adapted Mind*, ed. J. Barkow, L. Cosmides, and J. Toobey, 523 (Oxford: Oxford University Press, 1993).

7. Carl Sagan and Ann Druyan, *Shadows of Forgotten Ancestors* (New York: Ballantine, 1992), 370.

8. Carl Sagan, *The Dragons of Eden* (New York: Ballantine, 1977), 95.

9. Jay Appleton, *The Experience of Landscape*, rev. ed. (London: Wiley, 1996). Appleton modestly presented his thoughts as only a hypothetical framework for further development. That framework, however, has been empirically substantiated: directly by John Archea ("Visual Access and Exposure," Ph.D. diss., Pennsylvania State University, 1984), Stephen Kaplan ("Aesthetics, Affect, and Cognition," as in n. 1), and D. M. Woodcock ("A Functionalist Approach to Environmental Preference," Ph.D. diss., University of Michigan, 1982); and indirectly by Gordon Orians and Judith Heerwagen ("Evolved Responses to Landscapes" [as in n. 6]). (Kaplan substantiates the prospect but finds no empirical support for the refuge; in fact he finds a negative correlation. The other scholars support the duality, however, and Kaplan's work on mystery, cited in Chapter 3, indirectly supports the refuge-prospect duality.) Appleton's position is also anticipated by others, Darwin himself of course, but also the authors cited in the Bibliography and many others as well.

10. Charles Dickens, *Bleak House* (New York: Norton, 1977), 28.

11. Appleton, *The Experience of Landscape* (as in n. 9), 103.

12. Woodcock, "Functionalist Approach to Environmental Preference" (as in n. 9).

13. Alois Riegl, *Stilfragen*, 23–24, as cited in Joseph Rykwert, *On Adam's House in Paradise* (New York: Museum of Modern Art, 1972), 32.

14. On this point see especially Oleg Grabar, *The Alhambra* (Cambridge, Mass.: Harvard University Press, 1978).

15. Kaplan, "Aesthetics, Affect, and Cognition" (as in n. 1), 3.

16. See e.g. Roger Ulrich, "Aesthetic and Affective Response to Natural Environment," in *Behavior and the Natural Environment,* ed. I. Altman and J. F. Wohlwill, 104–5 (New York: Plenum, 1983), for a summary of empirical work on this point.

17. Ulrich, "Biophilia, Biophobia, and Natural Landscapes" (as in n. 4), 90.

18. John Ruskin, *Modern Painters* (London: Cook and Wedderburn, 1912), 5:199–200.

19. Some scholars, notably Sir Alistair Hardy and Elaine Morgan, propose an aquatic phase in human evolution as the most likely explanation for several unique features in our physiology; see A. C. Hardy, "Was Man More Aquatic in the Past?" *New Scientist* 7:642–45; and Elaine Morgan, *The Aquatic Ape* (London: Souvenir Press, 1982). For a supportive commentary, see Graham Richards, *Human Evolution* (London: Routledge and Kegan Paul, 1987), 193–204; for a balanced evaluation see Daniel Dennett, *Darwin's Dangerous Idea* (New York: Touchstone, 1996), 243–45.

20. Herman Melville, *Moby Dick* (New York: Random House, 1930), 3. To this same point Marc-Antoine Laugier presents

> man in his earliest origins, without any other help, without other guide than the natural instinct of his needs. He wants a place to settle. Beside a tranquil stream he sees a meadow; the fresh turf pleases his eye, the tender down invites him. He approaches; and reclining on the bright colors of this carpet he thinks only of enjoying the gifts of nature in peace; he lacks nothing, he desires nothing; but presently the sun's heat begins to scorch him, and he is forced to look for shelter. A neighboring wood offers the cool of its shadows, he runs to hide in its thicket; and he is content again.
>
> (Quoted in Rykwert, *On Adam's House in Paradise* [as in n. 13], 43.)

21. Philip Thiel, Ean Duane Harrison, and Richard S. Alden, "Perception of Spatial Enclosure as a Function of the Position of the Architectural Surfaces," *Environment and Behavior* 18, no. 2 (Mar. 1986), 227–43.

22. This quotation and the two that follow are from Beatriz Colomina, "Intimacy and Spectacle: The Interior of Loos," in *Strategies in Architectural Thinking,* ed. John Whiteman, Jeffrey Kipnis, and Richard Burdett, 69–71 (Cambridge, Mass.: MIT Press, 1992). I am grateful to Claus Seligmann for bringing this essay to my attention. Although the author never uses the words "refuge" and "prospect," her discussion is about exactly those characteristics as manifested in the interiors of Loos's houses. Her discourse calls to mind a passage in a paper by Mary Ann Kirkby entitled "A Natural Place to Play," written for the Department of Landscape Architecture, University of Washington, 1984:

> When asked why his hiding spot should have an opening, Ryan, aged four, answered "Because I would need to see if you were coming." And on another occasion, when asked twice why he preferred one landscape over another, he answered, very matter of factly, "Because I could see." When asked why it was important to see he responded, without hesitating, "Because there might be wolves out there."

23. Nikolaus Pevsner, *Pioneers of Modern Design* (Harmondsworth: Penguin, 1960), 191.

24. Jay Appleton, *The Experience of Landscape* (as in n. 9), 103.

25. Norris Kelly Smith has observed that "a spacious openness exists around and in front of the building but not . . . behind and beyond it. The house is made to appear at once embraced by its natural setting and opened to it." Norris Kelly Smith, *Frank Lloyd Wright* (Englewood Cliffs, N.J.: Prentice-Hall, 1966), 77.

26. With Wright's later Hollyhock House, on a bare Los Angeles hill, such a planting program was carried out with Wright's enthusiastic approval, to make the building look like the drawing; he later urged such a scheme on Mr. and Mrs. Paul Hanna in Palo Alto, California, without success.

27. Kaplan, "Aesthetics, Affect, and Cognition" (as in n. 1), 3.

28. Philippe Boudon, *Lived-in Architecture*, trans. Gerald Onn (Cambridge, Mass.: MIT Press, 1979). Boudon praises the houses for the ease with which the vast majority have accepted extensive remodeling. No doubt that is praiseworthy, although one is also entitled to question the validity of an architecture that must be changed in considerable degree, at considerable effort and expense, to be acceptable for its purpose; surely part of the architect's task is to provide a building in which remodeling is not only possible but also largely unnecessary.

29. Ibid., 83.

30. The offices received a First Honor Award from the Seattle Chapter of the American Institute of Architects, November 1997.

31. Renee Jankuski, "A Hospice for Life"; and Cheryl Smith, "The Injury of Abuse: A Child's Healing through an Architectural Means," both design projects, Department of Architecture, University of Washington, 1995.

32. See e.g. Mary Victoria Porter, "The Role of Spatial Quality and Familiarity in Determining Countryside Landscape Preference," master's thesis, University of Washington, 1987.

33. Judith H. Heerwagen and Gordon H. Orians, "Humans, Habitats, and Aesthetics," *The Biophilia Hypothesis*, ed. Stephen R. Kellert and Edward O. Wilson, 151–53 (Washington, D.C.: Island Press, 1993).

34. I am aware that "darkness" is not the physicist's terminology. I use it deliberately nevertheless because it seems a clearer way to describe an experiential characteristic with which we are all familiar; and I find I have support in this usage from, among others, my colleague Professor Marietta Millet, a noted authority on lighting.

35. It has not been my purpose in this book, or in my prior one, to eulogize Wright. But I am struck yet again by the accuracy of his intuition in this matter of the value of darkness as in so many other matters, and the degree to which his zones of darkness suggest those of the Japanese spaces he admired so much.

3. Exploring

1. Stephen Kaplan, "Aesthetics, Affect, and Cognition," *Environment and Behavior* 19, no. 1 (Jan. 1987): 8.

2. Ibid.

3. Stephen Kaplan, "Perceptions and Landscape," 1979, in *Environmental Aesthetics*, ed. Jack L. Nasar, 50 (Cambridge: Cambridge University Press, 1988).

4. Gordon H. Orians and Judith H. Heerwagen, "Evolved Responses to Landscapes," in *The Adapted Mind*, ed. J. Barkow, L. Cosmides, and J. Toobey, 509 (Oxford: Oxford University Press, 1993).

5. "Into the Uncharted: Eric Owen Moss's House in Los Angeles," *Progressive Architecture* (May 1993): 73.

6. This discussion refers only and entirely to the Islamic portions of the mosque.

7. The reconstruction is controversial, but I consider it here from an experiential point of view as an extant artifact, whether designed by Daedalus or Evans or both.

8. It has long been argued that Abbot Suger, whose rebuilding of the east end of the Abbey of Saint-Denis is generally agreed to be the first manifestation of the Gothic, was obsessed by theological analogies of light and color; see e.g. Otto von Simson, *The Gothic Cathedral* (New York: Harper, 1956). A recent study by William Folkestad ("The Feretory Master of Saint-Denis," Ph.D. diss., University of Washington, 1993) tracing other projects by the Saint-Denis master mason, however, suggests that this mason, not Suger, was responsible for the large windows and many other features of the chevet.

9. Chartres is one of many exceptions to my claim in the introduction that it is usually possible to approximate three-dimensional reality through two-dimensional illustrations. A slide of Chartres seen on a screen can hint at the actuality, since the projected light can simulate the window's transmitted light — but the image occupies a small cone of vision, while the actuality surrounds. Ink on a page, as here, is still less adequate. Recent restoration of the glass has increased the light quantity, so the interior is now closer to its thirteenth-century state. Fair enough; but in my opinion the pre-restoration evidences of the vicissitudes of time were experientially advantageous.

10. Jay Appleton, *The Experience of Landscape*, rev. ed. (London: Wiley, 1996), 85–90.

11. Herman Melville, Moby Dick (New York: Random House, 1930), 76–77.

12. Jay Appleton, *How I Made the World* (Hull: University of Hull Press), 207.

13. Appleton, *The Experience of Landscape* (as in n. 10), 98 and 118.

14. Ibid., 99.

15. Ibid., 99–100.

16. This is an excerpt from taped comments by the son of a couple who built perhaps the last house to claim Wright's full personal involvement, in 1950–51. The son was twelve at the time of construction. His memories are not all positive. Nor is the commentary entirely clean data, for shortly before it was made, in 1986, he had heard my views on refuge and prospect in a symposium at Ann Arbor. In fact he follows the above sentences with: "Maybe that's, again, that refuge and prospect, or whatever the terms are." But I did not talk to him before he prepared this tape, and he prepared it for quite other purposes; his references to my talk, while supportive, make up no more than half a page in a twelve-page transcription; and he did not intend that I ever see the account.

17. Henry Adams, *Mont-Saint-Michel and Chartres* (Garden City, N.Y.: Doubleday, 1959), 1.

18. Ibid., 422.

19. I am grateful to Ziva Freiman, who, using some thoughts from my earlier book on Frank Lloyd Wright's houses (*The Wright Space* [Seattle: University of Washington Press, 1991]) as the basis for a critique of this house, to my knowledge first recognized and discussed the condition I have here termed interior peril ("Into the Uncharted: Eric Owen Moss's House in Los Angeles," *Progressive Architecture* 74, no. 5 [May 1993]: 68–77). In other respects Freiman interprets the stairway, and the totality as well, as a summation of characteristics whose architectural application was first discussed in *The Wright Space*, which she revises and extends to wider application:

> In the Lawson-Westen house, both prospect and refuge are internalized, an apt response to a mundane residential lot that offered little in the way of true prospects. The stair commands views of various parts of the house and grounds; the far vista of the ocean, available at roof level, is exploited to the full with the strong prospect/refuge qualities of the crow's nest, perched close to the truncated peak of the cone, which is open to the sky, yet enclosed by tall walls on three sides. . . . The dizzying quality of the stair structure also represents simulated danger—a familiar component of Moss's architecture, and one that jibes with the survival/pleasure hypothesis. Scads of children's books and movies, not to mention adult entertainment and sport, are based on the peculiar pleasure we take in being scared witless.

20. Joseph Campbell, *The Hero with a Thousand Faces* (Princeton, N.J.: Princeton University Press, 1949).

21. Kahn intended brick surfaces for this space. Whether they would have yielded the same interpretation of the experience is an open question; but the focus here is on what exists, not what was intended—the architectural experience, not the historical chronicle.

22. Vincent Scully, *Architecture* (New York: St. Martin's Press, 1991), 366.

4. Categorizing and Differentiating

1. Cited in Nicholas Humphrey, "Natural Aesthetics," in *Architecture for People*, ed. Byron Mikellides, 65 (London: Studio Vista, 1980).

2. William Wordsworth, "Preface to Lyrical Ballads," in *The Essential Wordsworth*, selections by Seamus Heaney (Hopewell, N.J.: Ecco Press, 1988), 85.

3. John R. Platt, "Beauty: Pattern and Change," in D. W. Fishe and John R. Madde, *Functions of Varied Experience* (Homewood, Ill.: Dorsey, 1961), 403; see also Peter F. Smith, "Urban Aesthetics," in Mikellides, ed., *Architecture for People* (as in n. 1), 84: "It is now widely accepted that the basis of aesthetic experience stems from the interaction between chance and order, complexity and redundancy."

4. Jay Appleton, *How I Made the World* (Hull: University of Hull Press, 1993), 193.

5. Steven C. Bourassa (*The Aesthetics of Landscape* [London and New York: Bellhaven Press, 1991],

88) offers as a critique of Gestalt theory: "Why should the brain be programmed to react in some specific way to certain abstract formal qualities of the landscape—such as order and complexity—in the absence of any functional basis for such reactions? Gestalt theory offers no answers to such questions, although this is not to say that answers do not exist." I believe provisional answers exist.

6. Some scholars claim such interpretations have been attached to the orders from their beginnings in early Greece, many centuries before Vitruvius, and claim that allusions in Greek literature support this view. I do not find any such allusions in Greek literature from Homer through Thucydides, which ought to cover the ground. Therefore I need to have chapter and verse cited on this point before I become a believer. On Vitruvius's views, however, there can be no doubt.

7. Certainly the columns express the bearing of weight; that this is readily perceived as analogous to the human form in a like circumstance is less clear. At Athens and Akragas (modern Agrigento) literal representations of the human figure are used as columns, but per se these can cut either way as evidence of anthropomorphic intention in the column. One can argue that such columns show that the Greeks saw figure and column as analogous. One can also argue to the contrary, that when they wished to suggest the human figure as a column, they did so clearly and unambiguously by using the human figure and did not see the column as making the point.

8. Gerd Sommerhoff, *Life, Brain, and Consciousness* (New York: North-Holland, 1990). I am indebted to Joseph Donnette-Sherman for bringing Sommerhoff to my attention in his master's thesis, "Client Communication and Psychobiology," University of Washington, 1991.

9. Sommerhoff, *Life, Brain, and Consciousness*, 100.

10. Ibid., 261.

11. On October 15, 1993, at Astoria, Oregon, Leonard Eaton presented to the Pacific Northwest Chapter of the Society of Architectural Historians a paper entitled "Fractal Geometry in the Late Work of Frank Lloyd Wright," in which he argued that the crucial feature of fractal geometry, namely identical shapes of parts at many differences of scale, is found in much of Wright's late work. He cited as his key example the William and Mary Palmer house in Ann Arbor, Michigan, of 1950–51, which repeats equilateral triangles at scales ranging from entry lamp glazing and light-admitting brick cutouts to the plan of the living room.

12. Carl Sagan and Ann Druyan, *Shadows of Forgotten Ancestors* (New York: Ballantine, 1992), 166.

13. This is more than some Homo sapiens, myself for example, can do.

14. Humphrey, "Natural Aesthetics" (as in n. 1), 65.

15. There is occasional precedent for the terms in architectural criticism, e.g. William J. R. Curtis, *Modern Architecture since 1900* (Englewood Cliffs, N.J.: Prentice-Hall, 1982), 303: "It is therefore insufficient to see Utzon as a mere follower of Aalto, though he did draw on Aaltoesque qualities of subtle ordering and spatial complexity."

16. Alois Riegl, *Stilfragen*, 30–41, as quoted in Joseph Rykwert, *On Adam's House in Paradise* (New York: Museum of Modern Art, 1972), 32.

17. Humphrey, "Natural Aesthetics" (as in n. 1), 69.

18. Henri Poincaré, "Mathematical Creation," in *The Creative Process*, ed. Brewster Ghiselin, 39–40 (Berkeley and Los Angeles: University of California Press, 1952).

19. Both Lincoln and Churchill made a study of prose style and phrasing; Churchill composed most of his more memorable speeches in a poetic format of lines and stanzas. Still, it seems likely that phrases like those I quote in the text usually come into being because the originator has what Strunk and White call "an ear," an intuitive ability to construct phrases possessing such patterns. Such an "ear" is typical of memorable orators; some of Kennedy's phrases come to mind, or Martin Luther King's "I have a dream," which, though brief, scans exquisitely. On Lincoln and the Gettysburg Address, see Garry Wills, *Lincoln at Gettysburg* (New York: Simon and Schuster, 1992); on Churchill see e.g. William Manchester, *Alone: 1932–1940*, vol. 2 of *The Last Lion: Winston Spencer Churchill* (Boston, Toronto, and London: Little, Brown, 1988). At the time of writing, however, Manchester's third volume, which presumably would include the Battle of Britain phrase, was not yet available: the analysis I offer here is my own.

20. Virgil, *The Aeneid*, trans. Robert Fitzgerald (New York: Vintage, 1990), 417. Fitzgerald, noting (416) that "many passages . . . embody or enact what they described or narrated," offers two examples:

> Intonuere poli, et crebris micat ignibus aether.

and

> Vertitur interea caelum et ruit Oceano nox,
> involvens umbra magna terramque polumque
> Myrmidonumque dolos. . . .

Of the first (1.90) he says, "Thunder rolls in the first half of the line, and an electric storm crackles in the second." Of the second (2.250ff) he remarks that "the density of echoing sounds conveys the density of this darkness."

21. I am indebted to my college friend and recent correspondent Marguerite Winter for many of these thoughts and words, though I must emphasize that any misinterpretations and misunderstandings are my fault, not hers.

22. The work on this material cited in my introductory comments (151 n. 3) that tested preferences for natural as compared with fabricated settings chosen for high visual quality shows this to be true; this view of the Alhambra was one such selected setting. I would not yet maintain that the results are definitive, but the provisional conclusion is supported by Mary Victoria Porter, "The Role of Spatial Quality and Familiarity in Determining Countryside Landscape Preference," master's thesis, University of Washington, 1987.

23. My wife and I live in a condominium unit in downtown Seattle that was originally identical to

perhaps forty others in the building. We remodeled our unit extensively. Ours is a topic of conversation among others who live in the building, especially those with units having the same original layout, not so much for its features as for its differences from the norm. Visitors to our apartment who also live in the building seem less interested in the precise differences between our unit and theirs than in the existence of significant differences itself.

24. Stephen Kaplan, "Aesthetics, Affect, and Cognition," *Environment and Behavior* 19, no. 1 (Jan. 1987): 10.

25. Robert Venturi, Denise Scott Brown, and Steven Izenour, *Learning from Las Vegas*, rev. ed. (Cambridge, Mass.: MIT Press, 1977).

26. Architecture may have played a direct role in this musical development. The earliest architectural setting for the Cluniac chant would have been Cluny II of ca. 950, which Kenneth Conant believes may have been vaulted. If so, it would have held each individual chanted note for a long time; one of my students timed a note in such a space and found it audible eight seconds after striking. Given a reasonable alacrity of pace in singing, such a space would keep several sequential notes audible at any one time — hence a suggestion of multiple simultaneous notes. The pioneer twelfth-century composers of homophonic and polyphonic music, Léonin and Pérotin especially, may have worked in a similar space, an earlier Notre-Dame de Paris.

27. For this discussion I am indebted to Peter Collins, "Genius Loci," *Progressive Architecture* 44, no. 7 (July 1963): 100–106, especially 104–6. He says (104), "These plazas are the classic historical examples of successful urban spaces; yet I have never yet seen any precise explanation of how the success was achieved, nor do I know of any author who clearly indicates that the whole sequence of facades is one of the most subtle examples of deliberate archaization ever built." Collins does so. For him, however, "the basic civic building around which all the others were consecutively assembled was the Doge's Palace"; I take the position that the palace was itself a response to the chapel. Nor does Collins mention the Logetta.

28. Smith, "Urban Aesthetics" (as in n. 3).

29. Vincent Scully long ago argued that the "refinements" of the Greek orders were intended to be perceived as enlivening elements (*The Earth, the Temple, and the Gods* [New Haven, Conn.: Yale University Press, 1960]). This discussion of the Parthenon could easily be extended to the other buildings on the site.

30. It may not be necessary that the reconstruction be true to the complete original. At Whitby Abbey, for example, I am conscious of completing, "in the mind's eye," the end wall of the nave, since most of it still remains; but I am not conscious of rebuilding in my mind the south wall, evidenced only in foundations. At the Basilica of Constantine, however, the spring points of the great central vaults can be discerned by those who look for them and can lead the imagination to "reconstruct" that space — and, by the way, to feel astonishment at it.

31. On this point see especially Platt, "Beauty: Pattern and Change" (as in n. 3).

32. Roger Ulrich, however, notes that "even high-complexity natural scenes can be efficiently processed, provided that the complexity is structured." Roger S. Ulrich, "Aesthetic and Affective Response to Natural Environment," in *Behavior and the Natural Environment*, ed. I. Altman and J. F. Wohlwill, 98 (New York: Plenum, 1983). Ulrich repeats the point in a different format on p. 105. There is also at least one current effort toward measuring complexity in urban and architectural material: see Ryuzo Ohno, "A Method of Measurement for Visual Complexity in the Environment" (progress report on ongoing research, Kobe University, Japan, 1995).

33. It may not have been so originally. Recent research, especially at Amiens, supports the long-standing suspicion that a good bit of medieval masonry was painted, and in bright colors too. Since we deal here with our own responses in the present day, however, such issues of historical accuracy are not central to the discussion.

34. Robert Venturi, *Complexity and Contradiction in Architecture* (New York: Museum of Modern Art; distributed by Doubleday, 1966), 25.

35. Of course architecture is not alone here. James Joyce felt an urge to explain at length the order behind *Ulysses*; and there is the fashion in painting amusingly, but not entirely erroneously, ridiculed by Tom Wolfe in *The Painted Word*.

36. Humphrey, "Natural Aesthetics" (as in n. 1), 65.

Some Closing Comments

1. I have come to think that Wright's career marks a watershed in this matter. In the Heurtley house in Oak Park, Illinois, of 1902 he put major spaces on the top floor under the roof, and in nearly all of his subsequent projects, large and small, he kept them there. He then devised structural alternatives to the crossties of gable and hip roofs, so spaces could open into those volumes for the spatial contrast essential to the prospect-refuge juxtaposition. He came on the scene at a time—the late nineteenth century—when large expanses of glazing were possible at acceptable cost, and he used these to achieve significant differences in light quantity between low small spaces and high expansive ones. Where one leads, however, others may follow, and opportunities are now available to all to explore and exploit these characteristics.

2. Testing of preferences for the golden section goes back to 1876 and generally substantiates such a preference, though the results are not entirely conclusive, and there is some indication that the preference is culturally based. Few have speculated about the cause of such a preference. One of the most interesting efforts is J. Benjafield and J. Adams-Webber, "The Golden Section Hypothesis," in *The British Journal of Psychology* 67 (1976): 11–14, but in treating the golden section as linear rather than geometric, it suggests no relationships to architecture. In testing at the University of Washington in 1992, 1993, and 1995, we could not establish that the golden section is either perceived or preferred; it should be

163

noted that a large number of the subjects were of Asian birth or ancestry. Because each sampling was small and our methodology may be vulnerable to professional critique, I am not prepared to claim that the results are solidly defensible.

3. Gordon H. Orians and Judith H. Heerwagen, "Evolved Responses to Landscapes," in *The Adapted Mind*, ed. J. Barkow, L. Cosmides, and J. Toobey, 513 (Oxford: Oxford University Press, 1993).

4. Robert MacLaury, "Prototypes Revisited," *Annual Review of Anthropology* 20 (1991): 60.

5. Carl Sagan, *The Dragons of Eden* (New York: Ballantine, 1977), 191.

6. Stephen Kaplan, "Aesthetics, Affect, and Cognition," *Environment and Behavior* 19, no. 1 (Jan. 1987): 15.

Adams, Henry. *Mont-Saint-Michel and Chartres.* Garden City, N.Y.: Doubleday, 1959.

Alcock, John. *Animal Behavior: An Evolutionary Approach,* 6th ed. Sunderland, Mass.: Sinauer, 1997.

Altman, I., and J. F. Wohlwill. *Behavior and the Natural Environment.* New York: Plenum, 1983.

Appleton, Jay. *The Experience of Landscape.* Rev. ed. London: Wiley, 1996.

———. *How I Made the World: Shaping a View of Landscape.* Hull: University of Hull Press, 1993.

———. *The Symbolism of Habitat: An Interpretation of Landscape in the Arts.* Seattle: University of Washington Press, 1990.

Archea, John. "Visual Access and Exposure: An Architectural Basis for Interpersonal Behavior." Ph.D. diss., Pennsylvania State University, 1984.

Bachelard, Gaston. *The Poetics of Space.* Translated by Maria Jolas. Boston: Beacon Press, 1964.

Barkow, J., L. Cosmides, and J. Toobey, eds. *The Adapted Mind.* Oxford: Oxford University Press, 1993.

Benedikt, Michael. *Deconstructing the Kimbell.* New York: Sites/Lumen, 1991.

Boudon, Philippe. *Lived-in Architecture: Le Corbusier's Pessac Revisited.* Translated by Gerald Onn. Cambridge, Mass.: MIT Press, 1979.

Bourassa, Stephen C. *The Aesthetics of Landscape.* London and New York: Bellhaven Press, 1991.

Brill, Michael. "Using Archetypes in the Design of 'Charged' Places." Paper written for the Horace W. S. Cleveland Fellowship of the landscape architecture program, University of Minnesota, 1989.

Campbell, Joseph. *The Hero with a Thousand Faces.* Princeton, N.J.: Princeton University Press, 1949.

Collins, Peter. "Genius Loci: The Historical Continuity of Cities." *Progressive Architecture* 44, no. 7 (July 1963).

Colomina, Beatriz. "Intimacy and Spectacle: The Interior of Loos," in *Strategies in Architectural Thinking,* edited by John Whiteman, Jeffrey Kipnis, and Richard Burdett. Cambridge, Mass.: MIT Press, 1992.

Dawkins, Richard. *The Blind Watchmaker.* London: Longmans, 1986.

Dennett, Daniel C. *Darwin's Dangerous Idea: Evolution and the Meanings of Life.* New York: Touchstone, 1996.

Dewey, John. *Art as Experience*. New York: Pentagon, 1934.

Dickens, Charles. *Bleak House*. New York: Norton, 1977.

Donnette-Sherman, Joseph Michael. "Client Communication and Psychobiology." Master's thesis, University of Washington, 1991.

The Essential Wordsworth, selections by Seamus Heaney. Hopewell, N.J.: Ecco Press, 1988.

Fishe, D. W., and John R. Madde, eds. *Functions of Varied Experience*. Homewood, Ill.: Dorsey, 1961.

Folkestad, William. "The Feretory Master of Saint-Denis: An Inquiry into the Origins of the Gothic." Ph.D. diss., University of Washington, 1993.

Frampton, Kenneth. *Modern Architecture: A Critical History*. London and New York: Thames and Hudson, 1992.

Freiman, Ziva. "Into the Uncharted: Eric Owen Moss's House in Los Angeles." *Progressive Architecture* 74, no. 5 (May 1993): 68–77.

Frisch, Karl von. *Bees: Their Vision, Chemical Senses, and Language*. Ithaca, NY: Great Seal Books, 1950.

Ghiselin, Brewster, ed. *The Creative Process*. Berkeley and Los Angeles: University of California Press, 1952.

Gombrich, E. H. *The Sense of Order: A Study in the Psychology of Decorative Art*. Oxford: Phaidon Press, 1984.

Grabar, Oleg. *The Alhambra*. Cambridge, Mass.: Harvard University Press, 1978.

Greene, Graham. *The Ministry of Fear*. London: Penguin, 1963.

———. *The Power and the Glory*. London: Penguin, 1962.

Hardy, A. C. "Was Man More Aquatic in the Past?" *New Scientist* (Mar. 1960): 642–45.

Hersey, George. *The Lost Meaning of Classical Architecture*. Cambridge, Mass.: MIT Press, 1988.

Hildebrand, Grant. *The Wright Space: Pattern and Meaning in Frank Lloyd Wright's Houses*. Seattle: University of Washington Press, 1991.

Jastrow, Robert, ed. *The Essential Darwin*. Boston: Little, Brown, 1984.

Jaynes, Julian. *The Origin of Consciousness in the Bicameral Mind*. New York: Houghton Mifflin, 1976.

Kaplan, Stephen. "Aesthetics, Affect, and Cognition: Environmental Preference from an Evolutionary Perspective," *Environment and Behavior* 19, no. 1 (Jan. 1987): 84–90.

Kaplan, Stephen, and Rachel Kaplan. *The Experience of Nature: A Psychological Perspective*. Cambridge: Cambridge University Press, 1989.

Kellert, Stephen R., and Edward O. Wilson, eds. *The Biophilia Hypothesis*. Washington, D.C.: Island Press, 1993.

Kirkby, Mary Ann. "A Natural Place to Play: Use of Refuge in a Pre-School Play Yard." Paper written for the Department of Landscape Architecture, University of Washington, 1984.

Lieberman, Philip. *The Biology and Evolution of Language*. New York: Macmillan, 1984.

Lipman, Jonathan. "Consecrated Space." In *Frank Lloyd Wright: A Primer on Architectural Principles*, edited by Robert McCarter. Princeton, N.J.: Princeton University Press, 1991.

MacLaury, Robert. "Prototypes Revisited." *Annual Review of Anthropology* 20 (1991): 55–74.

Manchester, William. *Alone: 1932–1940*, vol. 2 of *The Last Lion: Winston Spencer Churchill*. Boston, Toronto, and London: Little, Brown, 1988.

Melville, Herman. *Moby Dick.* New York: Random House, 1930.

Mikellides, Byron, ed. *Architecture for People.* London: Studio Vista, 1980.

Morgan, Elaine. *The Aquatic Ape: A Theory of Human Evolution.* London: Souvenir Press, 1982.

Nasar, Jack L., ed. *Environmental Aesthetics: Theory, Research, and Applications.* Cambridge: Cambridge University Press, 1988.

Orians, Gordon H., and Judith H. Heerwagen. "Evolved Responses to Landscape." In *The Adapted Mind*, edited by J. Barkow, L. Cosmides, and J. Toobey. Oxford: Oxford University Press, 1992, 555–79.

Porter, Mary Victoria. "The Role of Spatial Quality and Familiarity in Determining Countryside Landscape Preference." Master's thesis, University of Washington, 1987.

Richards, Graham. *Human Evolution.* London: Routledge and Kegan Paul, 1987.

Rykwert, Joseph. *On Adam's House in Paradise.* New York: Museum of Modern Art, 1972.

Sagan, Carl. *The Dragons of Eden.* New York: Ballantine, 1977.

Sagan, Carl, and Ann Druyan. *Shadows of Forgotten Ancestors.* New York: Ballantine, 1992.

Scully, Vincent. *Architecture: The Natural and the Man-Made.* New York: St. Martin's Press, 1991.

———. *The Earth, the Temple, and the Gods.* New Haven, Conn.: Yale University Press, 1960.

———. *The Shingle Style and the Stick Style.* New Haven, Conn.: Yale University Press, 1955.

Semper, Gottfried. *The Four Elements of Architecture and Other Writings.* Translated by Harry Francis Mallgrave and Wolfgang Herrmann. Cambridge: Cambridge University Press, 1989.

Simson, Otto von. *The Gothic Cathedral.* New York: Harper, 1956.

Smith, Norris Kelly. *Frank Lloyd Wright: A Study in Architectural Content.* Englewood Cliffs, N.J.: Prentice-Hall, 1966.

Sommerhoff, Gerd. *Life, Brain, and Consciousness.* New York: North-Holland, 1990.

Stern, Robert A. F. *Modern Classicism.* New York: Rizzoli, 1988.

Thiel, Philip, Ean Duane Harrison, and Richard S. Alden. "Perception of Spatial Enclosure as a Function of the Position of the Architectural Surfaces." *Environment and Behavior* 18, no. 2 (Mar. 1986): 227–43.

Venturi, Robert. *Complexity and Contradiction in Architecture.* New York: Museum of Modern Art; distributed by Doubleday, 1966.

Venturi, Robert, Denise Scott Brown, and Steven Izenour. *Learning from Las Vegas.* Rev. ed. Cambridge, Mass.: MIT Press, 1977.

Virgil. *The Aeneid.* Translated by Robert Fitzgerald. New York: Vintage, 1990.

Woodcock, D. M. "A Functionalist Approach to Environmental Preference." Ph.D. diss., University of Michigan, 1982.

Wright, Robert. *The Moral Animal.* New York: Vintage, 1995.

Designer
Nola Burger

Compositor
G&S Typesetters, Inc.

Text
10/15 Electra

Display
Univers Condensed
Bold and Light

Printer
Malloy Lithographing

Binder
John H. Dekker and Son